Into the Unknown

Catherine Allan
Sallie Harkness
James Love
Helen McLullich
Helen Murdoch

Oliver & Boyd

Acknowledgments

We are grateful to the following for giving permission to reproduce extracts from copyright works: The Bodley Head, from *Beowulf the Dragon Slayer* by Rosemary Sutcliff; Brandt and Brandt Literary Agents Inc, for 'Western Wagons' by Rosemary and Stephen Vincent Benet from *A Book of Americans* (Copyright 1933 by Rosemary and Stephen Vincent Benet. Copyright renewed © 1961 by Rosemary Carr Benet); Corgi Books, from *Amazing Facts about Prehistoric Animals* (© Victorama); J. M. Dent & Sons Ltd, from *The Borrowers* by Mary Norton; J. M. Dent & Sons Ltd, Granada and Watson, Little Ltd, from *The Indian in the Cupboard* by Lynne Reid Banks; Faber & Faber Ltd, from *Dog Days and Cat Naps* by Gene Kemp, for two illustrations by Carolyn Dinan from *Dog Days and Cat Naps* and for 'Nessie' by Ted Hughes (from *Moon Bells and Other Poems*, published by Chatto & Windus); Nicholas Fisk, for 'The Thieves of Galac' from *Sweets from a Stranger* (© Nicholas Fisk 1982, published by Puffin Books 1984); Lutterworth Press, from *The Desperate Journey* and *Mountain Rescue Dog* by Kathleen Fidler; Victor Gollancz Ltd, from *The White Horse Gang* by Nina Bawden; Hodder & Stoughton Ltd, from *Call-Out* by Hamish MacInnes and *Children on the Oregon Trail* by Anne Rutgers Van der Loeff; Macmillan, London and Basingstoke, for 'Two's Company' by Raymond Wilson from *Rhyme and Rhythm* (Yellow Book); Edwin Morgan, for 'The Loch Ness Monster's Song' from *Poems of Thirty Years* (Carcanet, Manchester, 1982); Oxford University Press, from *Scottish Folk-Tales and Legends* retold by Barbara Ker Wilson (1954) and for 'Five-Inch Tall' by Norman Nicholson from *The Candy-Floss Tree: poems by Gerda Mayer, Frank Flynn and Norman Nicholson* (1984); Penguin Books Ltd, from *Prehistoric Animals*, translated by Ruth Day (Frederick Warne Ltd 1975, p. 36. English translation © 1975 by Frederick Warne Ltd): Franklin Watts Inc. from *The Oregon Trail* by Walter Havighurst (copyright © 1960).

We are also grateful to the following for supplying photographs and giving permission for their use: Associated Newspapers (pp. 76–7); Peter Bell (p. 52); John Cleare/Mountain Camera (pp. 48, 50); Robert Harding Picture Library (p. 56); The Mansell Collection (p. 11); Scottish Tourist Board (pp. 76–7).

Illustrated by Shirley Bellwood, Linda Birch, Martin Camm, Robert Geary, Donald Harley, Nicholas Hewetson, Annabel Large, Eric Rowe, Lesley Smith, Pat Tourret, Barry Wilkinson and Joanna Williams

Oliver & Boyd
Longman House
Burnt Mill
Harlow
Essex CM20 2JE
An Imprint of Longman Group UK Ltd

First published 1986
Seventh impression 1993

ISBN 0 05 003850 8

© Oliver & Boyd 1986

Set in 12/16pt Monophoto Plantin 110
Produced by Longman Singapore Publishers Pte Ltd
Printed in Singapore
SWT/07

Contents

Two's Company

They said the house was haunted, but
He laughed at them and said "Tut, Tut!
I've never heard such tittle-tattle,
A ghost that groans and chains that rattle;
And just to prove that I'm in the right,
Please leave me here to spend the night."

They winked absurdly, tried to smother
Their ignorant laughter, nudged each other,
And left him just as dusk was falling
With a hunchback moon and screech owls calling –
Not that this troubled him one bit;
In fact, he was quite glad of it,
Knowing it's every sane man's mission
To contradict all superstition.

4

But what is that?   Outside it seemed
As if chains rattled, someone screamed!
Come, come, it's merely nerves, he's certain
(But just the same he draws the curtain).
The stroke of twelve – but there's no clock!
He shuts the door and turns the lock
(Of course, he knows there's no one there,
But no harm is done by taking care!);
Someone's outside – the silly joker
(He may as well pick up the poker).
That noise again!   He checks the doors,
Shutters the windows, makes a pause
To seek the safest place to hide –
(The cupboard's strong – he creeps inside).
"Not that there's anything to fear,"
He tells himself, when at his ear
A voice breathes softly, "How do you do!
I am the ghost.   Pray, who are you?"

RAYMOND WILSON

5

Ghost Story

Bring out the tall tales now that we told by the fire as we roasted chestnuts and the gaslight bubbled low. Ghosts with their heads under their arms trailed their chains and said "whooo" like owls in the long nights when I dared not look over my shoulder; wild beasts lurked in the cubby-hole under the stairs where the gas-meter ticked.

And I remember that we went singing carols once, a night or two before Christmas Eve, when there wasn't the shaving of a moon to light the secret, white-flying streets. At the end of a long road was a drive that led to a large house, and we stumbled up the darkness of the drive that night, each one of us afraid, each one holding a stone in his hand in case, and all of us too brave to say a word.

We reached the black bulk of the house.

"What shall we give them?" Dan whispered. "'Hark the Herald'? 'Christmas comes but Once a Year'?"

"No," Jack said. "We'll sing 'Good King Wenceslas'. I'll count three."

One, two, three, and we began to sing, our voices high and seemingly distant in the snow-felted darkness round the house that was occupied by nobody we knew. We stood close together, near the dark door.

Good King Wenceslas looked out
On the Feast of Stephen.

And then a small, dry voice, like the voice of someone who has not spoken for a long time, suddenly joined our singing: a small, dry voice from the other side of the door: a small, dry voice through the keyhole. And when we stopped running we were outside *our* house; the front room

was lovely and bright; the gramophone was playing; uncles and aunts sat by the fire; I thought I smelt our supper being fried in the kitchen.   Everything was good again and Christmas shone through all the familiar town.

"Perhaps it was a ghost," Jim said.

"Perhaps it was trolls," Dan said, who was always reading.

"Let's go in and see if there's any jelly left," Jack said.   And we did that.

DYLAN THOMAS

Do You Believe?

The three friends sat at ease round the glowing embers of a winter fire. They chatted quietly together, enjoying the warmth of the darkening room while, outside, the wind howled at the corners of the window frames. A shutter, its rusty hinges creaking in protest, swung loose from its catch and the wind crept under the door. The cat, which had been curled up by the fire, flattened its ears, rose to its feet and arched its back. The house fell suddenly silent. The conversation stopped and from somewhere up above, in the depths of the hushed house, the friends heard a muffled thumping sound. The dying embers of the fire sprang into life once more and the flickering light from the flames lit up the faces of the three friends.

"Do you believe in ghosts?" asked the first.

"Yes, *I* do!" replied the second. "I remember visiting that old manor house once – you know the one I mean –

just off the lane.   The house was empty at the time.
Empty, that is, except for my friend and me.   Well,
suddenly, without saying a word to each other, we
both had exactly the same feeling.   We were sure there
was someone else in the room.   We couldn't *see* anyone,
mind you, but the air positively tingled.   We couldn't
stand it.   We just bolted!   I've heard of other people
who've walked along that lane at night and been struck by
a mysterious hand.   No one to be seen – just a hand that
came out of the air!"

   "A ghostly hand?   I don't believe it!" said the third
friend.   "There's a perfectly simple explanation for both
of your stories. You and your friend just imagined a
strange presence in that 'empty' room.   Houses that are
supposed to be haunted are usually in lonely places – like
that manor house.   Most people get the creeps when
they're on their own.   It's human nature.   So they start
imagining all sorts of things....   As for those people being
hit on the head – that was probably a tawny owl that
didn't like them passing its nest.   Owls will do that
sometimes.   Because those people didn't know about owls
they were frightened and made up the story about an
invisible hand – just like people long ago thinking that
marsh-gas was something magical and calling it Will-o'-
the-Wisp!   And another thing – those noises we heard just
now – that was probably the water pipes.   They often
make a thumping kind of sound."

   "I'm not sure," said the first friend, staring thoughtfully
into the dancing flames.   "I don't think you can ever be
one hundred per cent certain about anything."

The Green Lady

There was surprise and concern when it was learned that Lady Jean Drummond of Newton Castle had secretly married one of the sons of the Blair family from the neighbouring Ardblair Castle. How could the young lovers hope to have any happiness when their families had been involved for many years in a bitter feud?

The concern turned to dark mutterings when Lady Jean disappeared immediately after the marriage, without trace or known reason. Rumour and superstition took over, and a legend grew up around this 14th-century tragedy that Lady Jean's green wedding dress had put her in the power of the Water Kelpies who had spirited her away.

Since then, many people have had their summer afternoon disturbed by the ghost of a young lady, dressed in green, sitting at the window of the long gallery in Ardblair. She never tries to frighten anyone, yet her ghostly manner can send shivers down your spine, even in summer, as she flits along corridors, moving noiselessly from one room to another.

However, not all ghosts would seem to appear in lonely houses or ruined castles. People have reported seeing ghosts in the strangest of places. Here are but a few.

The Man in Grey

Audiences at the Drury Lane Theatre in London used to see a special visitor from time to time.

This was no ordinary theatre-goer. He wore a grey coat and breeches, hat, wig, riding boots and a sword. For more than two centuries actors and audiences saw this Man in Grey emerge from a wall in the upper circle, walk silently behind seats as onlookers gaped in awe, then vanish into the opposite wall.

Who was he? Where did he come from? Why was he there? No one knew. But in 1840 the body of a murdered man had been found, bricked up behind the wall from which the ghostly figure kept appearing.

Captain Towns' Ghost

One evening in 1873, in Sydney, Australia, Captain Towns' daughter walked into a bedroom in the family home where the pale light of a gas lamp dimly lit up the room. She gasped as she gazed at the wardrobe. Reflected in its shiny surface was a 'portrait' of her father, his thin, pale face and grey flannel jacket being unmistakable.

In a hushed voice she haltingly called on other members of the family, who came running to see what had disturbed her. The Captain's reflection was still there and the family watched as Miss Towns reached out to touch the image. Before she could do so the 'portrait' faded and died away, just as Captain Towns had died six weeks previously.

Just in time

In Detroit, USA, there is a factory worker who is convinced that he owes his life to a ghost.   It happened like this:

No one in the factory noticed that a huge press had been set moving by accident, and no one noticed that it was bearing down on a worker, and about to crush him to death.   No one, that is, except a tall, scarred, black man who dived forward with perfect timing to push the worker to safety.

"That fellow saved your life," exclaimed a colleague who rushed to the aid of his shaken friend.   But the Good Samaritan was nowhere to be seen or found.

Several people recognised his description.   It fitted a black man who had been killed at that spot twenty years earlier.

The Headless Hunter

Sam looked at Abe wonderingly. Of course Abe was exceptionally brave and daring, but surely everyone was scared of Gibbet Wood?

Abe laughed. "Me? Scared?" He thrust his hands into the pockets of his sagging trousers and hitched them up with a contemptuous swagger. "What's there to be scared of? I've been there hundreds of times – thousands, just about."

Sam whispered, "Have you seen the Headless Hunter, then?"

"Who's scared of an ole ghost?"

"Me," Sam would have answered if he had been honest. Instead he said, weakly, "Well, I s'pose there's no chance in the daytime."

The Hunter only rode at night, and only when the moon was hidden behind cloud. It was on one such night, long ago, that the Hunter had been riding home: the hunt had killed a long way off, near Caer Caradoc, and it was dark before he rode back, over the Bent Hill. He had been skirting Gibbet Wood when his horse was frightened by something – legend did not say what that something was, but perhaps even then Gibbet Wood was a place to fear – and his horse had bolted, running wild into the wood, under the low, sweeping branches, with the Hunter helpless on its back.

A low branch had snapped his head off, clean, like a sword. A farmer had found it, the long hair tangled in a tree, the eyes wide and staring. The body was never found, nor was the horse.

No one Sam knew had ever seen the Hunter's ghost but plenty claimed to have heard his horse thundering by.

Sam said, "You c'n feel him, like a sort of cold wind. And the hooves come on and don't stop – they sort of ride *through* you."

He shivered with pleasurable excitement. The Headless Hunter was not such a bad thing to think about, even to frighten yourself with, when the sun was hot and the sky was blue.

Now you see it — !

Certainly, Abe was not scared as Sam would have been. He was used to loneliness and was as much at home in the fields and woods after dark as a badger or a fox. Ordinarily, the night held no terrors for him.

But tonight was not ordinary. Once the mist had closed about him, he began to feel not frightened, exactly, but uncomfortable. The mist dampened all the sounds – cows champing, trees creaking, the rustling of small animals in the hedgerows – that would normally have made the country night familiar. All he could hear was the sound of his own footsteps, squeaking on the wet grass. When he stood still and listened, there was nothing else: he was alone in a silent, white world.

It was the silence that began to make him afraid. He dared not even whistle to keep his courage up.

Something loomed out of the mist and he broke into a cold sweat – colder than the chilling mist about him. But it was only a cow that lifted her head and gazed at him with brown, mournful eyes.   His relief was heartfelt.   "Oy, oy," he shouted and clapped her on her bony rump, but when she lumbered off into the mist, he was alone again.

He began to fear he might lose his way.   He knew every field, every rocky outcrop on the Bent Hill, but things seemed to change in the mist, become strangely shaped or insubstantial.   Here was the cob-nut tree – but was it *the* cob-nut tree?   Hands were a better guide than eyes tonight.   He closed his eyes and felt the trunk, sliding his hand up to the familiar fork just above his head.   Yes, it was the tree, all right: a little further and he would come to the edge of the wood.   Once there, all he had to do was to skirt it, keeping it always on his right hand side.

All the same, he was reluctant to leave the tree. It seemed friendly and solid.   He lingered, but the increasing chill, seeping through his tattered clothes, drove him onwards in the end.

Higher up it grew windier.   The mist distorted the sound of the wind in the trees and turned it into a booming noise, a foghorn sound, hollow and lonely.   The mist became thinner in some places and thicker in others. There was no constancy about it: it would suddenly lift as if some unseen hand had raised a curtain, revealing a bush ten yards away, every twig distinct and glistening, and then, before Abe reached it, the mist would descend again.

He pushed on doggedly.   Now he was at the edge of the
wood: briars lifted from the ground and caught at his legs,
unseen branches twanged against his face and showered
him with water drops.   He set his teeth and stumbled
down hill a little, away from the wood.   The wind seemed
to have dropped and there was now no sound at all.

No sound – and then he heard it: a drumming noise, so
faint at first, that only sharp ears could catch it.   Abe
heard it and stood still.   It was the thudding of hooves on
turf.   His breath stabbed sharply in his throat as he stood,
cold and listening.   He couldn't make out where it was
coming from, ahead of him or behind?   And then,

suddenly, it seemed to be all around him, a terrible drumming sound that made his heart stand still and the sweat break out on his forehead again. "The *Hunter*," he breathed. He remembered all Sam had told him – all that he had dismissed as kid's talk, just kid's talk. Now he feared it was true. Why, he felt so cold, it was as if he had turned to ice.

The hooves came closer and closer. The sound seemed to fill the world. He gave a little choked moan and put his hands over his eyes. "Don't let me see him," he prayed inwardly. "Just don't let me *see* him..."

Something bumped him between the shoulder blades and almost threw him down. With a wild cry he turned, arms flung wide...

It was the white horse. As he stared at her, joyously, unbelievingly, she bumped him again, gently, in the chest.

"Whitey," he whispered. "Oh Whitey, you must have known," he marvelled, wrapping his cold arms about her and burrowing his face into her warmly steaming neck. "You shouldn't be here, y'old fool. Not in someone else's field. I'll have to tether you up, that's what I'll have to do, or we'll be in a whole heap of precious trouble..."

He scolded her lovingly and she blew through her nose and lowered her head to crop the grass which was so much richer and greener than her legitimate pasture.

Abe tugged at her mane and called her gentle names, all the endearments he had never used to any other living creature. She was his own, his beauty, his good old mare, the only thing he loved or could remember loving since his Gran had bought her three years ago from the blacksmith at Long Broughton, who had said she was fit for nothing now, but the knacker's yard. "There, my lovely," Abe murmured as he scrambled on to her back and twined his hands in her long coarse mane. He dug his heels into her ribs. "Git on now," he said.

They jogged comfortably along. She had no bridle and Abe could not guide her, except with his knees, but she seemed to know her way home. He would have to be careful that she did not wander in future, Abe thought. Farmers did not take kindly to other people's animals trespassing on their grazing land. It was lucky there was a mist tonight. No one could have seen her. He sighed with relief and sat, slackly hunched, in the hollow of her back.

Lulled by her steady motion, he was nodding, on the edge of sleep, when she stopped still. He stiffened, yawning and rubbing his knuckles in his eyes. He grumbled, "Git on, Whitey. I'm starved cold . . ."

But she didn't move. Her ears were pricked up and pointing straight ahead.

"There's nothing there," Abe said, but as soon as he spoke he knew this was not true. He could hear the drumming hooves again, not loud this time but insistent and, terrifyingly, not only outside his head but inside it, too. Frantic, he beat his feet on the old mare's sides. She began to move, reluctantly at first, and then breaking into an untidy trot. "Giddup," Abe urged her in a whisper, but she seemed unable to go faster. Unable – or unwilling? Could she hear the drumming too? She shied suddenly – at nothing, it seemed. Abe looked up

and just ahead of him, at the very edge of Gibbet Wood, the mist lifted and he saw – for the rest of his life he swore to it – the horse standing there with its terrible rider, motionless, headless, staring. Then the mist came down and horse and rider vanished like a dream. Abe cried out, once, and his voice echoed back from the mist as from a wall. The white mare gathered herself beneath him and then stretched out in a slow, clumsy canter.

Abe lay on her back, half-fainting, and she carried him safely home.

From *The White Horse Gang*
by Nina Bawden

Colonel Fazackerley

Colonel Fazackerley Butterworth-Toast
Bought an old castle complete with a ghost,
But someone or other forgot to declare
To Colonel Fazack that the spectre was there.

On the very first evening, while waiting to dine,
The Colonel was taking a fine sherry wine,
When the ghost, with a furious flash and a flare,
Shot out of the chimney and shivered, "Beware!"

Colonel Fazackerley put down his glass
And said, "My dear fellow, that's really first class!
I just can't conceive how you do it at all.
I imagine you're going to a Fancy Dress Ball?"

At this, the dread ghost gave a withering cry.
Said the Colonel (his monocle firm in his eye),
"Now just how you do it I wish I could think.
Do sit down and tell me, and please have a drink."

The ghost in his phosphorous cloak gave a roar
And floated about between ceiling and floor.
He walked through a wall and returned through a pane
And backed up the chimney and came down again.

Said the Colonel, "With laughter I'm feeling quite weak!"
(As trickles of merriment ran down his cheek).
"My house-warming party I hope you won't spurn.
You *must* say you'll come and you'll give us a turn!"

At this, the poor spectre — quite out of his wits —
Proceeded to shake himself almost to bits.
He rattled his chains and he clattered his bones
And he filled the whole castle with mumbles and moans.

But Colonel Fazackerley, just as before,
Was simply delighted and called out, "Encore!"
At which the ghost vanished, his efforts in vain,
And never was seen at the castle again.

"Oh dear, what a pity!" said Colonel Fazack.
"I don't know his name, so I can't call him back."
And then with a smile that was hard to define,
Colonel Fazackerley went in to dine.

CHARLES CAUSLEY

I to Eye

Arrietty lives with her parents, Pod and Homily Clock, under the floorboards of Great-Aunt Sophy's house. They are one of the few remaining families of Borrowers, a race of tiny people who live on the lost and discarded items that the human race overlooks.

On this occasion, Arrietty has been allowed to go with her father on a 'borrowing' expedition, and is enjoying the rare treat of being allowed to play in the fresh air, when suddenly she has a frightening experience.

Arrietty watched Pod move away from the step and then she looked about her. Oh, glory! Oh, joy! Oh, freedom! The sunlight, the grasses, the soft, moving air and half-way up the bank, where it curved round the corner, a flowering cherry-tree! Below it on the path lay a stain of pinkish petals and at the tree's foot, pale as butter, a nest of primroses.

Arrietty threw a cautious glance towards the front door-step and then, light and dancey, in her soft red shoes, she ran towards the petals. They were curved like shells and rocked as she touched them. She gathered several up and laid them one inside the other . . . up and up . . . like a card castle. And then she spilled them. Pod came again to the top of the step and looked along the path. "Don't you go far," he said after a moment. Seeing his lips move, she smiled back at him: she was too far already to hear his words.

A greenish beetle, shining in the sunlight, came towards
her across the stones.   She laid her fingers lightly on its
shell and it stood still, waiting and watchful, and when she
moved her hand the beetle went swiftly on.   An ant came
hurrying in a busy zig-zag.   She danced in front of it to
tease it and put out her foot.   It stared at her, non-
plussed, waving its antennae; then pettishly, as though put
out, it swerved away.   Two birds came down, quarrelling
shrilly, into the grass below the tree.   One flew away, but
Arrietty could see the other among the moving grass stems
above her on the slope.   Cautiously she moved towards
the bank and climbed a little nervously in amongst the
green blades.   As she parted them gently with her bare
hands, drops of water plopped on her skirt and she felt the
red shoes become damp.   But on she went, pulling herself
up now and again by rooty stems into this jungle of moss
and wood-violet and creeping leaves of clover.   The
sharp-seeming grass blades, waist high, were tender to the
touch and sprang back lightly behind her as she passed.

When at last she reached the foot of the tree, the bird
took fright and flew away and she sat down suddenly
on a gnarled leaf of primrose.   The air was filled with
scent.   "But nothing will play with you," she thought and
saw the cracks and furrows of the primrose leaves held
crystal beads of dew.   If she pressed the leaf these rolled
like marbles.   The bank was warm, almost too warm here

within the shelter of the tall grass, and the sandy earth smelled dry.   Standing up, she picked a primrose.   The pink stalk felt tender and living in her hands and was covered with silvery hairs, and when she held the flower, like a parasol, between her eyes and the sky, she saw the sun's pale light through the veined petals.   On a piece of bark she found a wood-louse and she struck it lightly with her swaying flower.   It curled immediately and became a ball, bumping softly away downhill in amongst the grass roots.   But she knew about wood-lice.   There were plenty of them at home under the floor.   Homily always scolded her if she played with them because, she said, they smelled of old knives.   She lay back among the stalks of the primroses and they made a coolness between her and the sun.   And then, sighing, she turned her head and looked sideways up the bank among the grass stems. Startled, she caught her breath.   Something had moved above her on the bank.   Something had glittered. Arrietty stared.

It was an eye.   Or it looked like an eye.   Clear and bright like the colour of the sky.   An eye like her own but enormous.   A glaring eye.   Breathless with fear, she sat up.   And the eye blinked.   A great fringe of lashes came curving down and flew up again out of sight.   Cautiously, Arrietty moved her legs; she would slide noiselessly in among the grass stems and slither away down the bank.

"Don't move!" said a voice, and the voice, like the eye, was enormous but, somehow, hushed – and hoarse like a surge of wind through the grating on a stormy night in March.

Arrietty froze. "So this is it," she thought, "the worst and most terrible thing of all: I have been 'seen'! Whatever happened to Eggletina will now, almost certainly, happen to me!"

There was a pause and Arrietty, her heart pounding in her ears, heard the breath again drawn swiftly into the vast lungs. "Or," said the voice, whispering still, "I shall hit you with my ash stick."

Suddenly Arrietty became calm. "Why?" she asked. How strange her own voice sounded! Crystal thin and harebell clear, it tinkled on the air.

"In case," came the surprised whisper at last, "you ran towards me, quickly through the grass . . . in case," it went on, trembling a little, "you scrabbled at me with your nasty little hands."

Arrietty stared at the eye; she held herself quite still. "Why?" she asked again, and again the word tinkled – icy-cold it sounded this time, and needle-sharp.

"Things do," said the voice. "I've seen them. In India."

Arrietty thought of her Gazetteer of the World.

"You're not in India now," she pointed out.

"Did you come out of the house?"

"Yes," said Arrietty.

"From whereabouts in the house?"

Arrietty stared at the eye. "I'm not going to tell you," she said at last, bravely.

"Then I'll hit you with my ash stick!"

"All right," said Arrietty, "hit me!"

"I'll pick you up and break you in half!"

Arrietty stood up. "All right," she said and took two paces forward.

There was a sharp gasp and an earthquake in the grass; he spun away from her and sat up, a great mountain in a green jersey. He had fair, straight hair and golden eyelashes. "Stay where you are!" he cried.

Arrietty stared up at him. So this was 'the boy'!

From *The Borrowers*
by MARY NORTON

Five-Inch Tall

I'm five-inch tall.
I dive and crawl
Into the jungle
Of the uncut lawn.
Fawn-coloured stems
Of plate-size daisies
Sway round my head
In a tangle of weed.
A monstrous, pop-eyed,
Dinosaur snail
Stares out from the dome
Of his mobile home,
Leaving a slime-trail
Wide as a drain.
In distant, dark-furred
Thickets of twitch,
A cricket whirs
Like a motor-mower.

I creep from the lower
Foothills of lawn
Into a conifer
Forest of horse-tails,
Where writhing, boa-
constrictor worms
Coil round fern-trunks
Or heave through the soil.

Undaunted, unshaken,
I break from the shade
To a lake of sunlight –
Five-inch tall
And the heir of acres,
With all the walled dukedom
To call my own.

But high on a pear tree
A pocket falcon,
With bragging, flaunted,
Red-flag breast,
Is poised to strike;
Dives down and pounces –
Grappling-iron talons
And beak like a pike.
Shaken, daunted,
Arms over my chest,
I cringe and turn tail;
Off like a shot
To the vegetable plot,
Helter-skelter for the shelter
Of broccoli and kale;
Yielding the field
To red-rag robin –
For safety is all
When you're five-inch tall.

NORMAN NICHOLSON

Birthday Presents

It was not that Omri didn't appreciate Patrick's birthday present to him.   Far from it.   He was really very grateful – sort of.   It was, without a doubt, *very* kind of Patrick to give Omri anything at all, let alone a second-hand plastic Red Indian which he himself had finished with.

The trouble was, though, that Omri was getting a little fed up with small plastic figures, of which he had loads.   Biscuit-tinsful, probably three or four if they were all put away at the same time, which they never were because most of the time they were scattered about in the bathroom, the loft, the kitchen, not to mention Omri's bedroom and the garden.

Gillon, his other brother, hadn't bought him anything because he had no money (his pocket-money had been stopped some time ago in connection with a very unfortunate accident involving their father's bicycle).   So when Gillon's turn came to give Omri a present, Omri was very surprised when a large parcel was put before him, untidily wrapped in brown paper and string.

"What is it?"

"Have a look.   I found it in the alley."

The alley was a narrow passage that ran along the bottom of the garden where the dustbins stood.   The boys used to play there sometimes, and occasionally found treasures that other – perhaps richer – neighbours had thrown away.   So Omri was quite excited as he tore off the paper.

Inside was a small white metal cupboard with a mirror in the door, the kind you see over the basin in old-fashioned bathrooms.

You might suppose Omri would once again be disappointed, because the cupboard was fairly plain and, except for a shelf, completely empty, but oddly enough he was very pleased with it. He was not a very tidy boy in general, but he did like arranging things in cupboards and drawers and then opening them later and finding them just as he'd left them.

That night Omri put the cupboard on his bedside table, and opening it, looked inside thoughtfully. What would he put in it?

"It's supposed to be for medicines," said Gillon. "You could keep your nose-drops in it."

"No! That's just wasting it. Besides I haven't any other medicines."

"Why don't you pop this in?" his mother suggested, and opened her hand. In it was Patrick's Red Indian. "I found it when I was putting your trousers in the washing-machine."

Omri carefully stood the Indian on the shelf.

"Are you going to shut the door?" asked his mother.

"Yes, and lock it."

He did this and then kissed his mother and she turned the light out and he lay down on his side looking at the cupboard. He felt very content. Just as he was dropping off to sleep his eyes snapped open. He had thought he heard a little noise ... but no. All was quiet. His eyes closed again.

In the morning there was no doubt about it.   The noise actually woke him.

He lay perfectly still in the dawn light staring at the cupboard, from which was now coming a most extraordinary series of sounds.   A pattering; a tapping; a scrabbling; and – surely? – a high-pitched noise like – well, almost like a tiny voice.

To be truthful, Omri was petrified.   Who wouldn't be? Undoubtedly there was something alive in that cupboard. At last, he put his hand out and touched it.   He pulled very carefully.   The door was tight shut.   But as he pulled, the cupboard moved, just slightly.   The noise from inside instantly stopped.

He lay still for a long time, wondering.   Had he imagined it?   The noise did not start again.   At last he cautiously turned the key and opened the cupboard door.

The Indian was gone.

Omri sat up sharply in bed and peered into the dark corners.   Suddenly he saw him.   But he wasn't on the shelf any more, he was in the bottom of the cupboard.   And he wasn't standing upright.   He was crouching in the darkest corner, half hidden by the front of the cupboard.   And he was alive.

Omri knew that immediately.   To begin with, though the Indian was trying to keep perfectly still – as still as Omri had kept, lying in bed a moment ago – he was breathing heavily.   His bare, bronze shoulders rose and fell, and were shiny with sweat.   The single feather sticking out of the back of his headband quivered, as if the Indian were trembling.   And as Omri peered closer, and

his breath fell on the tiny huddled figure, he saw it jump to its feet; its minute hand made a sudden, darting movement towards its belt and came to rest clutching the handle of a knife smaller than the shaft of a drawing pin.

Neither Omri nor the Indian moved for perhaps a minute and a half. They hardly breathed either. They just stared at each other. The Indian's eyes were black and fierce and frightened. His lower lip was drawn down from shining white teeth, so small you could scarcely see them except when they caught the light. He stood pressed against the inside wall of the cupboard, clutching his knife, rigid with terror, but defiant.

The first coherent thought that came into Omri's mind as he began to get over the shock was, "I must call the others!" – meaning his parents and brothers. But something (he wasn't sure what) stopped him. Maybe he was afraid that if he took his eyes off the Indian for even a moment, he would vanish, or become plastic again, and then when the others came running they would all laugh and accuse Omri of making things up. And who could blame anyone for not believing this unless they saw it with their own eyes?

Another reason Omri didn't call anyone was that, if he was not dreaming and the Indian had really come alive, it was certainly the most marvellous thing that had ever happened to Omri in his life and he wanted to keep it to himself, at least at first.

His next thought was that he must somehow get the Indian in his hand. He didn't want to frighten him any further, but he *had* to touch him. He simply had to. He reached his hand slowly into the cupboard.

The Indian gave a fantastic leap into the air. His black pigtail flew and the air ballooned out his loose-fitting leggings. His knife, raised above his head, flashed. He gave a shout which, even though it was a tiny shout to match his body, was nevertheless loud enough to make Omri jump. But not so much as he jumped when the little knife pierced his finger deeply enough to draw a drop of blood.

Omri stuck his finger in his mouth and sucked it and thought how gigantic he must look to the tiny Indian and how fantastically brave he had been to stab him. The Indian stood there, his feet, in moccasins, planted apart on the white-painted metal floor, his chest heaving, his knife held ready and his black eyes wild. Omri thought he was magnificent.

"I won't hurt you," he said. "I only want to pick you up."

The Indian opened his mouth and a stream of words, spoken in that loud-tiny voice, came out, not one of which Omri could understand. But he noticed that the Indian's strange grimace never changed – he could speak without closing his lips.

"Don't you speak English?" asked Omri. All the Indians in films spoke a sort of English; it would be terrible if his Indian couldn't. How would they talk to each other?

The Indian lowered his knife a fraction.

"I speak," he grunted.

Omri breathed deeply in relief. "Oh, good! Listen, I

don't know how it happened that you came to life, but it
must be something to do with this cupboard, or perhaps
the key – anyway, here you are, and I think you're great, I
don't mind that you stabbed me, only please can I pick you
up?   After all, you are my Indian," he finished in a very
reasonable tone.

He said all this very quickly while the Indian stared at him. The knife-point went down a little further, but he didn't answer.

"Well? Can I? Say something!" urged Omri impatiently.

"I speak *slowly*," grunted the miniature Indian at last.

"Oh." Omri thought, and then said, very slowly, "Let – me – pick – you – up."

The knife came up again in an instant, and the Indian's knees bent into a crouch.

"No."

"Oh, *please*."

"You touch – I kill!" the Indian growled ferociously.

You might have expected Omri to laugh at this absurd threat from a tiny creature scarcely bigger than his middle finger, armed with only a pin-point. But Omri didn't laugh. He didn't even feel like laughing. This Indian – *his* Indian – was behaving in every way like a real live Red Indian brave, and despite the vast difference in their sizes and strengths, Omri respected him and even, odd as it sounds, feared him at that moment.

"Oh, okay, I won't then. But there's no need to get angry. I don't want to hurt you." Then, as the Indian looked baffled, he said, in what he supposed was Indian-English, "Me – no – hurt – you."

"You come near, I hurt *you*," said the Indian swiftly.

Omri had been half lying in bed all this time. Now, cautiously and slowly, he got up. His heart was thundering in his chest. He couldn't be sure why he was being cautious. Was it so as not to frighten the Indian, or because he was frightened himself? He wished one of his brothers would come in, or better still, his father ... But no one came.

Standing in his bare feet he took the cupboard by its top corners and turned it till it faced the window. He did this very carefully but nevertheless the Indian was jolted, and, having nothing to hold on to, he fell down. But he was on his feet again in a second, and he had not let go of his knife.

"Sorry," said Omri.

The Indian responded with a noise like a snarl.

There was no more conversation for the next few minutes. Omri looked at the Indian in the early sunlight. He was a splendid sight. He was about seven centimetres tall. His blue-black hair, done in a plait and pressed to his head by a coloured headband, gleamed in the sun. So did the minuscule muscles of his tiny naked torso, and the reddish skin of his arms. His legs were covered with buckskin trousers which had some decoration on them too small to see properly, and his belt was a thick hide thong twisted into a knot in front. Best of all, somehow, were his moccasins. Omri found himself wondering (not for the first time recently) where his magnifying glass was. It was the only way he would ever be able to see and appreciate the intricate embroidery, or beadwork, or whatever it was which encrusted the Indian's shoes and clothes.

Omri looked as closely as he dared at the Indian's face. He expected to see paint on it, war-paint, but there was none. The turkey-feather which had been stuck in the headband had come out when the Indian fell and was now lying on the floor of the cupboard. It was about as big as the spike on a conker, but it was a real feather. Omri suddenly asked,

"Were you always this small?"

"I no small! You, big!" the Indian shouted angrily.

"No – " began Omri, but then he stopped.

He heard his mother beginning to move about next door.

The Indian heard it too. He froze. The door of the next room opened. Omri knew that at any moment his mother would come in to wake him for school. In a flash he had bent down and whispered, "Don't worry! I'll be back." And he closed and locked the cupboard door and jumped back into bed.

"Come on, Omri. Time to get up."

She bent down and kissed him, paying no attention to the cupboard, and went out again, leaving the door wide open.

From *The Indian in the Cupboard*
by Lynne Reid Banks

The sun ruled the sky above the island.   The sea licked
about its shores, catching the light and glittering.   The sea
was the Aegean; the island, Crete.

   To Crete, across the sea, there fled a man called
Daedalus.   He was an engineer, the most brilliant inventor
of his time, but when the skill of his nephew, Talus, had
come near to rivalling his own, jealous Daedalus had
pushed him from a rooftop to his death.   As punishment,
he had been exiled from Athens, city of his birth.   He took
with him into exile his young son, Icarus, whom he loved
dearly.

   On Crete, at Cnossus, stood a palace, brilliant in the
sun.   Here on a throne inlaid with gold sat Minos, King of
Crete.   Before him even proud Daedalus came bowing
low.

   "Welcome, Daedalus, welcome to our court.   Your
name is known to us and also your skill.   We have a task
to meet such skill as yours."   Minos rose from his throne
and led Daedalus and Icarus to a door set with iron
bars.   From the room beyond came a warmth, a stench
like a farmyard.

   "We desire you to build us a stronghold beneath our
house from which nothing, from which no one can escape,
neither man nor monster – not even monsters so mighty, so
awful as this, the Minotaur, our son."

   Its hands that came to grasp the bars were huge, but

human hands with hair upon them curled and black,
each hair as thick, as stiff as wire.   Its limbs were
human-shaped though hard as wood.

It glared at Daedalus with red, small furious eyes, then
opened its cavernous red mouth and roared at him, flinging
back its head, the bludgeon head of a huge black bull.

Daedalus bowed to the king again.

"Great King, you are great indeed, but you could choose
no better architect than I.   The prison I construct will
make the names of Minos and Daedalus remembered for
the rest of time.   No man nor monster will be able to
escape from it."

Daedalus drew plans first, scratching them out on tablets of wax.   Then he set troops of slaves and labourers to work, enough men to make an army.   Deep beneath the palace, with picks and spades and hammers, they gouged out the rocks of Crete.   Some hacked and smashed at them till the sparks flew off.   Some carried the rubble away in baskets on their backs; yet others cut props and pillars to support the roof.

Little by little they tunnelled from the bitter rock a labyrinth, a maze of tunnels so intricate that anyone who entered without knowing its secret would never find his way out.

In the labyrinth lived the Minotaur.   When it roared people trembled for they knew that Minos sent those who angered him to feed his son.   Into it also were sent Athenian youths and girls to provide food for the monster.

A young Athenian, Theseus, hoped to kill the monster and offered himself as food for the Minotaur.   When he arrived in Crete, Ariadne, daughter of Minos, fell in love with him and begged Daedalus help her rescue him.

At Daedalus' suggestion she gave Theseus a ball of golden thread which he was to unwind as he penetrated the labyrinth so that he could retrace his steps.

He tied one end to the entrance and kept hold of the ball.   When he found the Minotaur he killed him and by means of the thread found his way out and escaped from Crete, taking Ariadne with him.

Guards came and seized Daedalus and Icarus.   They dragged them before Minos who was furious and bellowing like a bull, for he had discovered the Minotaur was dead and he was sure Daedalus had had a hand in the plot.

"So you boasted, Daedalus, that no one could escape from the labyrinth. The Minotaur is dead. A man has killed our son. He has understood the maze and sailed away unharmed from Crete. Now you and your son shall be cast into the maze and if you, too, escape from there, you'll get no further. Without ships no man can escape from Crete, and clever as you are, you command no ships upon our Aegean Sea."

So Daedalus, with his son, Icarus, was cast into the prison he had made.

After they had walked through many turns and windings they smelled a familiar farmyard reek. The stench went on growing all the time till they reached the cave at the heart of the labyrinth, where the corpse of the Minotaur lay rotting on dirty straw. It seemed feeble now. Its red eyes were closed, its limbs were limp. Only the yellow horns still looked dangerous. Daedalus gazed beyond it, shuddering, holding up his little lamp till its light reached the furthest corner of the cave, where human bones and skulls lay scattered everywhere. There were feathers also, from birds devoured by the Minotaur. He picked one up and examined minutely its shaft and quill.

"Minos rules the land of Crete," he said. "He may rule the sea that surrounds it too. But remember, Icarus, he does not rule the sky."

Icarus did not know what his father meant by this. He watched Daedalus lay feathers overlapping in four separate rows, each diminishing in size from one end to the other.

Then Daedalus brought forth from his tunic a cake of wax, a needle and some fine strong thread. He joined the larger feathers with the needle and thread. He softened the wax in the warmth of the lamp and used it to unite the small feathers.

Icarus watched his father's patient hands, watched small feathers waver in the heat above the lamp and the wax drip down in slow dull drops.

At last Daedalus took the completed rows, bent them and curved them into shape, and then his son could see what they were meant to be; how from the wings of birds, his father, Daedalus, had made wings for men, one pair each for himself and Icarus.

The oil of the lamp was all burned by now. As they left the cave, the wick flickered and went out. On and on they went in the darkness till at last the light broke suddenly, burst upon them. They had to bury their eyes against the blinding, burning sun.

When Daedalus' eyes accepted the light, he took some leather thongs and fixed the smaller pair of wings to the arms of Icarus. He fixed the larger to his own. They would have to use their arms just as the wing bones of a bird, making the feathers gently rise and fall.

"But mind, mind, Icarus, my son, don't fly too low, too near the sea, for the feathers once wet will not carry you. But then do not fly too high, too near the sun, for the sun's heat, like the lamp's, will melt the wax, make the feathers fall away."

Daedalus started to run along the hillside. When he had gained some speed he jumped into the air, shouting at Icarus to follow him. Both moved their arms with

awkward chopping strokes; they did not soar
as they had expected to, but struggled
jerkily, not far above the rock. Daedalus
kept close to Icarus, instructing him.

Icarus caught it first, the rhythm, the pattern of
flight. He swept into the air and away, filled with
joyfulness, shouting with delight, and almost at once
Daedalus followed him up into the sky. Their arms
flowed so smoothly up and down, the feathers took on such
life and force, that they did not seem like arms any more,
the bones felt fluid, supple. The air felt different too,
solid, protective, strong – it held, filled, surrounded them,
while above stood the golden beaming sun.

Higher and higher flew Daedalus and Icarus. Down below on land men began to notice them. When they flew across the sea, sailors came running to the sides of ships to stare at them.

Daedalus shouted to the air, the sun, the sea. He was the inventor of human flight, the first mortal man to fly. As he dreamed of his success he failed to watch the flight of Icarus.

Higher and higher flew Icarus towards the strengthening sun. The air grew hotter, the sun more brilliant, dazzling to his eyes. He had forgotten all warnings now, flying nearer as if drawn to it, like a moth towards a lamp.

Slowly the wax on his wings began to melt. It softened gently, then dripped a little, in slow thick drops. A feather slipped from it, fell drifting, turning, down towards the sea. Other feathers followed, singly at first, but then more and more of them at once. Although Icarus confidently moved his wings, there were not enough feathers left to hold the air, to keep him in flight.

His father looked back, to see his son plunge headlong towards the sea, but he did not swerve in safety like a gull above the glittering waves. He plunged right into the heart of them, and their startled waters closed above his head. All that remained of Icarus were some feathers floating on the sea, while his father flew, weeping, in the sky alone.

Mountain Medley

MOUNTAIN RESCUE

Tuesday January 4

CLIMBER SURVIVES 200 METRE PLUNGE

By Stuart Lindsay

A climber told yesterday how he escaped with only superficial injuries after falling 200 metres on Ben Nevis.

Mr Eammon McCarrol, 21, of Thorncliffe Gardens, Glasgow, was detained for ob―

Hospital, January 30

luckiest n

Mr Mc

holiday w

Ben Nevis

tempted th

Run on the

'I had ge

summit,' he

became soft

slab gave way

tumbling dow

luckiest I land

'I was terr

not know mu

happening.'

His fall had b

Kinloss mounta

Monday, January 10.

FEARS GROW FOR CLIMBERS AFTER RUCKSACKS FOUND

Fears for three climbers mounted last night after two rucksacks were found in the snow high in a Glencoe corrie.

Glencoe mountain rescue team led by Hamish M search yesterday failed to return Buachaille Etive night.

rted by helicopt checked s, and were di art hi

rs ar nput v, M n en ne e e

LOST CLIMBERS FOUND SAFE

Two climbers, missing for five hours after falling on Stobinian, a 1200 metre mountain near Crianlarich, were last night found alive by mountain rescue teams.

Earlier, an uninjured companion of the climbers had struggled down the snow-covered mountainside to raise the alarm.

Killin, Crianlarich, and Callander mountain rescue teams were alerted.

The man gave a position for the injured climbers, but when rescuers reached the spot these was no sign of them.

rch leader, Police Sergeant Callander,

ning by the oll, a local day: 'They

TAKE CARE

TAKE ADVICE
– from an experienced mountaineer. Competence on the hills can only come with guidance.

ADVISE SOMEONE OF YOUR ROUTE
– route cards are available at police stations, hostels etc.

KNOW THE MOUNTAIN CODE
– treat the hills with caution and respect.

EXTRA CLOTHING
– carry spare woollens and food.

CARRY MAP AND COMPASS
– know how to use them.

ALWAYS CHECK LOCAL WEATHER FORECASTS
– remember BAD weather is the normal on Scottish hills and good weather the exception.

RISKS ARE OUT
– the solo mountaineer can cause problems so never climb alone.

EXPERIENCE IS THE KEY
– plan carefully and do not over-estimate your own stamina or ability.

The Rescue
of Carolyn Knight

Hamish MacInnes is the leader of the Glencoe Mountain Rescue
Team and a well-known writer on mountaineering and rescue
techniques.   He tells the following story....

New Year is always a busy time in Glencoe when climbers
flock northwards to spend Hogmanay in the Glen.

It was at this season that Sandy Whillans called in to see
me and remarked speculatively, "Well, Hamish, I wonder
how many we'll take down over the next few days?"

"We should run a lottery on it," I suggested.
"Proceeds to go to the team."

"Aye, that's a good idea," answered Sandy, taking a long
pull on his pipe.

Sandy had just left the workshop when, at 3 p.m., the
telephone rang.   It was Dudley Knowles who, with his
wife Ann, had taken over the management of the Clachaig
Inn.

"There's a chap just come in, Hamish, who says his
girlfriend has fallen on Stob Coire nam Beith.   He thinks
she has a broken leg and says that there is a party of other
climbers up there with her."   Dudley didn't believe in
wasting words!

"Does she have any other injuries?" I asked.

"He says that she may also have injured her back," Dud
informed me after consulting with the lad.

I told him to ask Ann to put the call-out procedure

into operation and arrange for everyone to meet at Achnambeithach in fifteen minutes.

My rucksack was already packed with all the necessary equipment and first-aid; it was only a matter of putting my boots and snow gaiters on, then driving the few miles down the road to Achnambeithach.   Though it was cold, it was a good day; but I could see that the tops of the hills had that blurred, white look which indicates near-blizzard conditions on the summit.

When I arrived I went straight into our rescue truck and sorted out what would probably be required for this straightforward evacuation.   By the time I had finished, a few more of the team had arrived.   Dud and Sandy Whillans agreed to take turns with the stretcher whilst Alan Fyffe and I went on ahead with the casualty bag and first-aid equipment.   In these wintry conditions exposure is a grave risk, especially to the injured or anyone suffering from shock.

About 4 p.m. Alan and I reached the party of six climbers; the girl was covered in down jackets and anoraks. She was lying on a ledge which had been cut out of the ice; two of the climbers were holding her in position, with their ice-axes driven into the slope on the underside of her. Diagnosis of injuries in such conditions can be very difficult and this occasion was no exception; the wind had increased to full gale-force and the biting blast cut our faces like a knife. Spumes of snow, whipped up by the wind, cascaded from the ridge above. It was like being in a sand-blasting cabinet.

Though the injured girl, Carolyn Knight, could move her legs, she complained of bad pains in her ribs and back. I gave her some pain-killing tablets when we put her into the casualty bag. By this time, Sandy Whillans had arrived with the stretcher, dressed only in his pullover and climbing breeches as, lower down, he had given Dud Knowles all his personal gear to carry.

"Cripes, I'm cold," said Sandy. "It would freeze a brass monkey! ... How is she?" he added.

"Doesn't look too good," I replied. Carolyn was out of earshot and the wind whipped the words away in the opposite direction from where she lay. "But it's difficult to tell. I haven't had a good look at her yet."

I handed Sandy my anorak since I also had a duvet jacket. He was chilling very quickly after the seven hundred metre carry with the stretcher and had also hurt his back when he stumbled on his way up the icy section of the path.

We rapidly organised belays on the rock face above and,

after strapping Carolyn to the stretcher, we lowered her down the remainder of the slope on long ropes. It was 350 metres down for she had not fallen to the bottom but had lodged on some frozen scree which was responsible for her injuries.

We brought Carolyn off the hill with little incident and she was sent to the Fort William Hospital. We later learnt she had lost a great deal of blood and was given a transfusion but she recovered eventually.

Some six weeks after the incident, I received a letter from her boyfriend who was with her when she fell. In his letter he assured me that they were responsible climbers which, no doubt, they were. He also very generously suggested that he would deduct so much each week from his wages in appreciation of the Glencoe Mountain Rescue Team. Of course, we had to refuse this offer which might have caused him hardship. He did, however, send us a cheque for which we thanked him. It bounced! We never had the heart to let him know.

From *Call-Out*
by HAMISH MacINNES

Notice Board

MOUNTAIN RESCUE: TEAM'S EQUIPMENT

Team member's RUCKSACK should contain:

a) Map (and polythene bag)

b) Compass

c) Head Torch (plus spare bulbs and batteries)

d) Polythene bag (7' x 3')

e) Whistle

f) Spare dry clothing (in a polythene bag)

g) Food (e.g. chocolate and sweets)

h) First Aid equipment

i) Flares

j) Slings, spare short lengths of rope, bootlaces etc.

k) Knife

l) Balaclava helmet

m) Gloves

All this equipment must be kept clean and dry, and always serviceable. Failure of a battery on a mountainside may result in a serious accident!

<u>PLEASE CHECK</u>

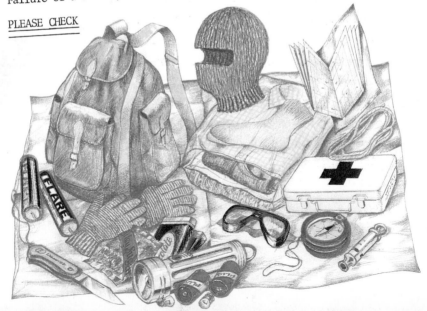

Avalanche

AVALANCHE is the name given to a sudden rush of lying snow which tumbles from a hillside.

In winter considerable amounts of snow fall on the mountains of Britain. When city streets are shining with rain, there may be a blizzard raging on the mountain tops. The snow which lies on the hillsides is in a constant state of change and avalanches are often released because of changes in the weather. The danger is greatest after a sudden thaw or during a heavy snowfall and up to 24 hours after it. Snow which lies on slopes of 14° and more can avalanche.

When going on the hills in winter, climbers should start early in the day when weather conditions are still cold enough to keep the snow stable. They should avoid climbing in steep gullies or crossing steep open slopes and should keep to buttresses and ridges as much as possible.

With more and more climbers and skiers using the mountains in winter the risk of avalanche has increased. Avalanches have become a major cause of winter accidents in the Scottish mountains.

Avalanches sweep their victims away, burying them in the snow. They may be buried deeply, or less than a metre from the surface. Sometimes the avalanche carries them quite a distance from the spot where they disappeared.

To search for victims, rescue workers use long sounding-rods which they push through the snow, hoping to feel

resistance when the rod touches a buried person.   This is
a slow laborious task and the longer a person is buried the
less his chance of survival.

Recently, dogs have been used in avalanche rescue.
Their keen sense of smell leads them quickly to where the
victim is buried.   Once the survivor has been located the
rescue workers can dig him out.

'Seek and Speak!'

Fiona Baird and Alex Moore had taken their Alsatian dogs, Candy
and Rory, to a training course in 'Search and Rescue' which was
being organised by Fiona's uncle James Macdonald. Fiona's mother
and Alex's father were also involved.

"This will do well enough," said James Macdonald,
pointing towards a gentle slope covered by a drift of
snow. "There's enough snow here. We are going to
tackle the first part of the Course. That's to train a dog to
look for people under the snow. Will you work in pairs,
please? Fiona, you work with your mother. Dr Moore
can partner Alex. Now the first thing each pair has to do
is to dig a hole in the bank of snow – about eighteen inches
deep. Make the hole big enough to hold two people. See
that your dogs are lying comfortably on their waterproof
sheets. They mustn't be allowed to dig with you at this
stage."

For a while, only the sound of spades could be heard.
The command 'Sit' had been given to all the dogs.
They sat at a distance and watched.

At last all the holes were dug, looking like shallow
graves.

"Now each owner must move back with the dog and his
assistant, about thirty-five paces from the hole," James
Macdonald instructed. "When you get there, face the
hole with your dog."

This was done and everyone was in position.

"Now, hand over the dog's leash to your assistant."

Fiona handed Candy's leash to her mother.

"Walk backwards to the hole, in full sight of the dog. The assistant must not allow the dog to follow you. As you go towards the hole, keep calling your dog's name. When you reach the hole, lie down in it."

Fiona and Alex plodded backwards, calling to their dogs as they went. The result was a babel of shouted names and eager barking, as the dogs strained to go after their masters.

"Now unleash the dogs but keep hold of their collars," James Macdonald ordered. "Point with your free hand towards the hole where the master is hiding and give the command, 'Seek! Seek!' Then let the dog loose, but run after it. Don't let it out of your sight, ever, on these exercises."

Mrs Baird had little need to point to Fiona's hiding place. On her command 'Seek! Seek!' she let go of Candy's collar and Candy bounded in Fiona's direction. As soon as she reached her, she began to lick her hands and face as though she had been lost for a long time.

"Reward your dogs with a tit-bit when they've found you. Let them get the idea that there will always be a reward when they find a person," James Macdonald said. Fiona felt in her pocket for the usual chocolate drop.

Rory had 'found' Alex easily too and was going through the same reward performance.

"That's fine for a beginning," Uncle James continued. "Now for the second exercise. Just a reminder though – always have the reward ready in a pocket. These dogs can only be trained by kindness. But give the reward only if the dog has done his exercise properly.   The dog must realise he *has* to do his part of the job first.   This time I want you to work in threes.''

"You work with Fiona and Mrs Baird, Alex," Dr Moore said.

When everyone was sorted into little companies of three, they were informed that this time the dog's master was to be *buried* in the snow.   A ripple of excitement ran through the group.   "Now don't get all of a jitter," said James. "We'll introduce you to this burial business stage by stage.   This time the master goes back with his helper to the hole he has already dug, while the third assistant holds on to the dog.   As the master goes towards the hole, he keeps calling the dog.   Then he lies down in the hole while his assistant covers him with a few inches of snow.   Don't press the snow down.   Leave it loose."

"How shall we breathe?" Alex asked.

"You'll breathe all right, Alex.   The snow is dry and loose, so there are pockets of air in it and little channels to the surface.   If you put your arms round your head that'll make another pocket of air.   There'll only be an inch or two of snow over you."

"Will it be very cold?" someone else asked.

"Not very.   You'll be surprised when you get under the snow how warm it can be.   It's more the thought of it that's shivery.   Anyone *not* want to go on with it?"

No one refused.

"Once the dog's owner is buried, the person who has buried him goes back to the starting place.   Then the third person lets the dog loose, giving it the command,

'Seek! Seek!' "

Alex held on to Candy while Mrs Baird went back to the hole.

As Fiona went away, she called, "Candy! Candy!" over her shoulder. Candy tugged her leash to get after her.

Once Fiona was under two or three inches of snow her mother said, "Uncle James once told me that people can hear under the snow, Fiona. If you can, show me by poking a finger through the snow."

Sure enough, Fiona's leather-gloved finger came up through the snow. Reassured, Mrs Baird went back to Alex. Candy was straining at the leash, desperate to go after Fiona.

"Go and find Fiona. Seek and speak!" Alex gave the command as he released the catch on the leash on Candy's collar.

Candy was away like the wind. She reached the place where Fiona had been lying on the previous occasion. She checked suddenly. No Fiona! She lifted her nose and gave a plaintive howl. She looked perplexed, but Fiona's scent still came to her. Fiona *must* be somewhere about. Candy sniffed at the blanket of snow that lay over Fiona. She caught a stronger scent, then she realised that Fiona was there, *under the snow*. Desperately she began to scratch and scrape with her paws, sending the snow flying in all directions, barking loudly at the same time.

"Candy's certainly got the idea of 'Seek and Speak'," Uncle James commented. He had been moving from group to group and had now reached his family. "This is the moment when we give the dog some help to dig out the owner."

He joined Alex and Mrs Baird at the burial hole, and they scraped away the snow. Fiona sat up, shaking the snow from her face and hair. Candy yelped with joy, and began licking her face.

"Good lassie, Candy!" Fiona praised her. "Hi! Steady up! Give me a chance to put my hand in my pocket."

Out came a chocolate biscuit this time.

The whole performance had to be repeated with Alex and Rory. This time Dr Moore helped to bury Alex while Fiona held Rory.

When she gave Rory the command and let him go, he rushed to the spot. Like Candy he checked when he did not find Alex. Rory seemed more taken aback than Candy had been. He ran about uncertainly, sniffing the air and whining. Fiona left Candy with her mother and went to help Rory.

"Go on, Rory! Seek and speak!" she encouraged him. Uncle James was watching closely, notebook in hand, to make his assessment. Rory stayed by the snow grave.

"Dig a bit with your hand at the grave, Fiona. Rory's found it, but he doesn't know what to do now. You can hear me, Alex. You give a shout for help."

Rory watched Fiona beginning to dig and he sniffed at the snow over Alex.

"Dig! Go on, Rory! Dig! Find Alex!" Fiona encouraged him.

Alex gave a muffled shout – "Help!" That convinced Rory that he was buried under the snow. As Candy had done, he began to scrape away the snow with his paws till he uncovered Alex's face and head.

"Hi! Watch out, Rory! Don't scratch my face!" Rory was all over Alex at once, licking wildly at his face and sending the snow flying in all directions.

"Don't forget to praise Rory and give him his reward," Uncle James reminded Alex as he scrambled out.

"How did you feel about being buried?" Alex said to Fiona. "Were you scared? I admit I was, a bit."

"So was I at first," Fiona confessed. "But once I was under the snow it was quite comfortable. It wasn't even as cold as I expected. It was quite *peaceful*. It was a bit eerie hearing you all tramping about overhead and speaking to each other and not being able to speak back."

"I was surprised that Rory heard me calling. It must have sounded very faint," Alex remarked.

"It did. Faint and muffled, as though you were a long distance away," Fiona said.

"If you had been buried deeper, we might not have heard you cry at all," Uncle James told Alex. "People who have been buried in avalanches tell us that it is a terrible thing when they are trapped under the snow; they can hear people walking and talking above them, but they cannot make themselves heard at all."

"How horrible for them!" Fiona gave a shudder.

"That's why we have to rely on the dog's sense of smell to find them. If the dogs dig, and bark loudly at the same time, that's the best chance the buried person has of being saved."

From *Mountain Rescue Dog*
by KATHLEEN FIDLER

Toothie and Cat

High on the hills above the city was a cave, well hidden away among the trees and the rocks and the bracken. And in that cave lived an old tramp with a gingery, greyish beard hanging to his waist, a greasy hat on his head, string tied just below the knees of his trousers and one tooth that stuck out over his beard. Because of this he was known as Toothie, and he couldn't remember any other name. Nobody had ever cared for him much ever since his mother dumped him, wrapped in a blanket, outside a police station, and then made off as fast as she could.

Below the hills in the city lived Cat. Cat the Black and the Bad, a streak of a cat with claws as sharp as daggers and a heart as black as his tatty fur. No one loved Cat. Once he was dropped in a river and left to drown. But you don't drown animals like Cat that easily. He got out, and survived, by hatred mostly. He hated people and children and bright lights and kindness. He loved fighting and stealing, rooftops and alleys and, most of all, dustbins. In the daytime he thieved and slept on walls in patches of sunlight. At night he rampaged across rooftops, wailing and caterwauling.

So he lived for some years, till one morning he dropped from a rooftop a bit carelessly, and a car speeding through the dawn grazed his leg. Snarling and swearing, he limped to the side of the road, where Toothie, who had also been raiding dustbins, found him. He was pleased for he'd found a very meaty bit of chicken carcase.

He walked all round Cat, who spat at him.   Then he popped a bit of chicken into the complaining mouth, and Cat stopped spitting and ate instead.   Toothie popped him

in his old bag and went back to the cave, where he made some chicken soup and tied a big leaf round the injured leg.   After a time Cat stopped spitting at him, for he'd grown to like Toothie's smell.   His leg healed.

Cat did not return to the city.   It was summer.   He hunted and Toothie cooked: stews and soups in his iron pot, other tasty dishes baked in mud packed at the base of the fire.

Long warm days passed by in the green wood and the dark cave.   Sometimes Toothie would sing and Cat purr, both rusty noises.   That autumn was beautiful, warm and golden, with more nuts than had been seen for years. Toothie and Cat were well fed and content.   Until

the night the October wind arrived, blowing cold,
stripping the leaves off the trees, and it brought with it the
sound of cats singing in the city below.   Cat stirred in his
sleep and woke up.   He left Toothie's warmth to sit in the
mouth of the cave, listening.   Yes, there, again, came the
yowling of cats.   Cat shivered.   He looked once at the old
man, asleep, and slipped out into the night.

A fortnight later he came back, hungry, limping, wet and
exhausted, longing for Toothie's warm fire, Toothie's food,
Toothie's smelly company.   But the cave was empty.
The iron pot hung forlornly by the burnt-out fire.
Toothie had gone.

Cat sat and washed himself, which is what cats do when
they don't know what to do next.   Then he searched
through the woods, crying his strange, wild call.   There
was no Toothie.   Cat slew an unwary bird who would
have done better to have migrated and, still hungry, set off
for the city.

Through the streets he ran, sniffing, investigating,
fighting, always searching for Toothie's fascinating smell,
and one day, a week or so later, he arrived at the City
Hospital and knew that his friend was inside.

Now Cat was much cleverer than Toothie, and he knew
from the smell of the hospital that that was where people
were ill, and his cat brain put illness and chicken together.
He'd got to find some chicken.

He tried as many houses as he had paws before he finally
crept into a gleaming, shiny, bright kitchen, and there on
the immaculate, tiled surface lay a scrumptious chicken leg
on a plate of crisp salad.   The salad Cat ignored, he was

not a lettuce-eater, but he seized the chicken and was just about to leap through the partially-opened window when the owner appeared, screamed like a whistling kettle and spent the rest of the day feeling very ill indeed, and telling anyone who could be made to listen how a fiendish monster had appeared like a black demon in her sacred kitchen. Cat kept increasing in size till he reached the dimensions of a mini-tiger.

A while later, the mini-tiger sat outside the hospital door and waited, chicken portion gripped firmly in teeth. Going in at the front door didn't seem like a good idea – it looked too busy and important. Cat had never liked front doors anyway. Back or side doors were for the likes of him. So he slunk round the corner till he came to a dark staircase that went up and up and on and on. Right at the top were dozens of dustbins. Cat purred through the chicken. He liked those dustbins, homely and friendly, they were.

Beyond them was a door with two little round glass panels. It opened in the middle and swung as someone walked through. And Cat slid in, keeping a very low profile. He ran, chicken in mouth, and stomach almost on the floor, through rows of beds, and then into another ward with yet more beds. In the third, a little boy lay in bed, bored. He sat up and cried:

"There's cat. It's got something in its mouth. Good ole puss cat. Come here."

He wanted Cat a lot, but Cat ran on. But now that he was spotted, pandemonium broke loose.

"Catch that cat!"

"Stop him!"

"Get that filthy animal out of here!"

As fast as he could, Cat ran on.   Patients shouted as nurses ran to grab him.

But nothing could stop Cat now.   Like a rocket swooshing into space, Cat shot down the ward to find Toothie.   He dodged trolleys, ran under beds, ran over beds, squeezed between legs, narrowly missed cleaners, tripped up nurses carrying vases of flowers or trays, scattering people right and left to reach the bed with the screens round it where Toothie lay dying.

He'd collapsed with pneumonia a week after Cat had left him and somehow, shivering, coughing, full of pains, he'd crawled to the road, where a bus driver had driven him

straight to the hospital despite complaints from some of the passengers. And since then, Toothie had lain in terror of the bright lights, the uniforms, the smells and the sounds, all too much for his mazed mind. He wanted to die.

Sister's voice rang out loud and clear.

"Stop that beast! It's got germs!"

Hands grabbed at Cat, missing narrowly. He shot through the screens and the doctor and nurses beside Toothie and up on to the bed. There on the whiter than white, brighter than bright, snowy, frosty, bleached, purified, disinfected, sterilised, decontaminated pillow, Cat laid the dusty, greasy, tooth-marked chicken leg, just beside Toothie's head. Shouts were all about him now.

But Toothie's eyes opened and he saw Cat. A triumphant burst of purring sounded through the ward. Come what might, Cat had arrived. He'd found Toothie.

From *Dog Days and Cat Naps*
by GENE KEMP

Morag and the Water Horse

When the warm days come and the sun begins to burn the
bracken brown, according to their age-old customs the
Highland crofters take their cattle to summer pastures in
the hills, re-opening the shielings where they will stay until
it is time to return home again.

Many years ago there lived a crofter called Donald
MacGregor, whose summer shieling lay on a lonely slope
of hill-side overlooking a great loch.   His little cabin
stood as a haven in the midst of the heather, and the lush
grass that grew on the lower land provided rich pasture for
his cattle.   And yet there were many people who shook
their heads and called Donald MacGregor a foolish man to
have built his shieling in that place; and there was no one
who would set out along the path that led there once dusk
had fallen upon the earth.   This was because a dreaded
monster lived in the depths of the great loch near by,
preying upon the hill-side round about: a Water Horse.

No man could describe the appearance of the
monster.   Those who had stayed long enough to catch
more than a glimpse of the terrible creature as it rose from
the dark waters of the loch had not lived to tell the tale;
while, as it roamed the hill-side, it was able to assume any
form at will (for it was full of evil enchantment) and might
appear as an aged woman, a black raven, or perhaps a
cunning-eyed fox, only resuming its own shape when it

was near enough to seize and mercilessly devour its prey. But it was said that the Water Horse was huge and black; that two sharp, satanic horns sprang from its monstrous head; and that it could outstrip the wind as it plunged through the heather.

But in spite of the tales that were told of this fearsome creature, and although each year the Water Horse claimed another victim for its own, Donald MacGregor took no notice when his neighbours warned him of the danger of having his shieling so near the loch, advising him to move across the burn that trickled by its side – for it was known that a Water Horse might never cross over running water, and all land beyond the burn was safe. Donald only replied that his cattle should have the richest pasture he could find for them, which happened to be on the very borders of the loch, and that he would believe in the existence of the Water Horse when he met it face to face. As for the monster's luckless victims, he swore that their disappearance was really due to the fact that they had availed themselves too freely of their neighbours' hospitality, and in the dark had stumbled and fallen over a precipice along their homeward path.

Yet in the end he was forced to take back his scornful words; and this is the way it happened.

Donald had one daughter called Morag, whom he loved dearly. Each year she used to accompany her father to their summer dwelling, and all through the long, light days she would sit at the door of the shieling with her spinning-wheel. Then, as approaching darkness deepened the purple shadows in the heather, she would go down to the

lochside to call in the cattle. As she went barefooted over
the hill, she told herself that there was nothing to fear; for
had not her father told her that she should not be afraid?
And yet she shivered as the waters of the loch lapped
against their grassy margins, and peered distrustfully into
the shadows cast by the rowan trees that grew there. But
always she returned safely, and in the daytime frightening
fancies fled away, and Morag would sing as she sat
spinning in the sun.

One golden morning as she was turning her wheel
without a care in the world, a dark shadow came between
herself and the sunlight, and she broke off her song with a
scream.

"I did not mean to startle you," said a pleasant voice;
and looking round, Morag discovered a young man
standing beside her. He was tall and comely, and there
was the look of strength on his broad shoulders. Yet his
appearance was strange, for his clothes and hair were dark
and dripping with water.

"How is it you are so wet?" asked Morag, "for there is
not a cloud to be seen in the sky."

"For sure," the young man answered easily, "the sole of
my foot slipped as I passed by a tarn high in the hills, and I
fell into the water. The sun will soon dry me."

He sat on the ground by Morag's side, and she was not loth to let her spinning-wheel stand idle while he spoke fair words to her. Yet in spite of the charm in his manner, his pleasant speech, and tender glances, Morag could not help feeling that there was something strange about him, although she tried to push this thought away from her mind.

As he felt the sunlight on his scalp, the young man brushed one hand over his damp head.

"Lay your head upon my lap," said Morag, "and let me smooth your hair."

And while the young man did as she bade him, she began to comb his dark locks with gentle hands, but suddenly she paused in her combing, and terror entered her soul.

Morag saw that the teeth of the comb were choked with fine green strands of weed and grains of silt. That weed and silt she knew well, for had she not seen it often in her father's net when he fished in the great loch below the hill-side? In truth it was the *liobhragach an lochan* that was wrapped round the roots of the young man's hair.... Young man? This was no young man, but the dreaded Water Horse itself, risen from its lair and present in this comely shape to lure her to her death.

At this moment the monster saw the great fear in Morag's eyes. With a terrible scream she pushed the dark head away from her and sprang to her feet. The spinning-wheel toppled to the ground as she fled away and away down that steep hill-side, with the wings of terror on the heels of her. And behind, dreadful in the sunlight, spread a great shadow that was darker than the deepest waters of the great loch itself.

But Morag was more fortunate than many another who had been marked out as a victim by the Water Horse, for the monster did not succeed in overtaking her before she reached the little burn that trickled by the side of the loch; and once she had leaped across its running water, she was

safely out of danger.

Never again did any man enter the door of the little shieling above that haunted loch – not even Donald MacGregor, who was so shaken by his daughter's peril that he took back every word he had ever spoken in derision of the Water Horse.   And to this day you may see the scattered stones of the ruined cabin lying in the midst of the curling bracken.

From *Scottish Folk Tales and Legends*
by Barbara Ker Wilson

The Mystery of the Loch

For generations the crofters of the Scottish Highlands
have passed stories on to their children about the great
beasts that are supposed to live in the lochs.
Best known of them all is the
Loch Ness monster.

Loch Ness is about 38 kilometres long – more than
the distance from Dover to Calais – and over 2
kilometres wide.   It is very deep, 240 metres, and the
cliffs around the sides drop sheer to the lake bed.
Millions of years ago it was an inlet of the sea.   Sea
creatures swam in and out to find good feeding, and to
shelter from enemies within the deep waters of the inlet.
  The land rose and the loch became an inland lake.
The sea creatures trapped in the loch were forced to
remain and breed there.   Today the only outlet to the
sea is the shallow River Ness and the Caledonian Ship
Canal.

Saint meets Monster

One of the first stories of the monster in Loch Ness was written 1400 years ago. We are told that Saint Columba was waiting to cross Loch Ness when he saw some people burying a dead man who had been bitten by a water monster. As Saint Columba's companion swam across the loch to fetch a boat moored on the opposite side, the ferocious monster emerged and came towards him. In a loud voice, the saint commanded the monster to go back and not to touch the man. The monster turned and fled away, frightened by his powerful voice.

Monster-Hunters

About 1527, we are told, a certain Duncan Campbell and several other men went monster-hunting. They went to the loch-side early one morning, and 'suddenly the monster did, without any force, overthrow huge oaks with his tail'. It killed three of the men with blows from its tail before it returned to the water. The terrified monster-hunters tried to hide in trees, without much success. The story is told in a *History of Scotland*, published in 1527. The tales that the crofters hand down all suggest that the monster is of uncertain temper and to be feared.

The old coach road along the loch was replaced in 1933 by a new motor road. The trees were cut down to give a good view of the loch. Now reports began to pour in from people who had seen a great beast on the surface of the loch. Most reports were of several humps moving across the water; others saw a small head and long neck.

In 1934 a local resident went home late one night. In the moonlight he noticed a large animal in the bushes. At his approach the creature took fright and lumbered across the road and into the loch at great speed.

Monster on film

There have been a few scientific expeditions. Tim Dinsdale, on his one-man expedition in 1960, obtained a film of a large creature swimming in the loch. Two expeditions have used boats equipped with echo-sounders. A party of Cambridge scientists, who led one of the expeditions, said results suggested that a large and unusual animal lived in the loch. Where would this large animal find food? Salmon and trout live in the loch, fish come up through the river and migrating eels pass through. Many eels stay in the loch and grow to a large size – splendid food for monsters.

What kind of monster is it? In the 1930s a group of school-children told their schoolmaster of a large and horrifying monster they had seen by the loch. Asked to describe it, they pointed to a plesiosaurus in a picture of prehistoric animals on the wall.

The Tradition

The Loch Ness monster is not unique. Loch Morar, Loch Shiel and many other Scottish lochs are reported to have beasts that appear infrequently. All these lochs must once have been inlets of the sea, and all are in remote areas. Ireland, too has its beasts. There is a tradition, surviving today, of the dreadful beast called the Wurrum. Half fish, half dragon, it lives in some of the mountain lakes. Reports of monsters also come from the deep mountain lakes in remote areas of Canada, Iceland and Siberia, and tales of monsters have been handed down from generation to generation.

Tales of monsters of these isolated regions might have remained in the realm of pure fantasy and legend if the road around Loch Ness had never been built. Now many people claim there is no monster in Loch Ness, but many more are uncomfortably sure there is.

From *Amazing But True*

Nessie

No, it is not an elephant or any such grasshopper.
It's shaped like a pop bottle with two huge eyes in the stopper.

But vast as a gasometer, unmanageably vast,
With wing-things like a whale for flying underwater fast.

It's me, me, me, the Monster of the Loch!
Would God I were a proper kind, a hippopot or croc!

Mislaid by the ages, I gloom here in the dark,
When I should be ruling Scotland from a throne in
   Regent's Park!

Once I was nobility – Diplodocus ruled the Isles!
Polyptychod came courting with his stunning ten-foot
   smiles.

Macroplat swore he'd carry me off before I was much older.
All his buddy-boys were by, grinning over his shoulder –

Leptoclid, Cryptocleidus, Triclid and Ichthyosteg —
Upstart Sauropterygs! But I took him down a peg —

I had a long bath in the Loch and waiting till I'd finished
He yawned himself to a fossil and his gang likewise
   diminished.

But now I can't come up for air without a load of trippers
Yelling: 'Look at the neck on it, and look at its hedge-
   clippers!
Oh no, that's its mouth.'   Then I can't decently dive
Without them sighing: 'Imagine! If *that* thing were alive!
Why, we'd simply have to decamp, to Canada, and at the
   double!
It was luckily only a log, or the Loch-bed having a bubble.

It was something it was nothing why whatever could it be
The ballooning hideosity we thought we seemed to see?'

Because I am so ugly that it's just incredible!
The biggest bag of haggis Scotland cannot swallow or sell!

Me, me, me, the Monster of the Loch!
Scotland's ugliest daughter, seven tons of poppycock!

Living here in my black mud bed the life of a snittery
   newty.
And never a zoologist a-swooning for my beauty!

O where's the bonnie laddie, so bold and so free,
Will drum me up to London and proclaim my pedigree?

TED HUGHES

Astonishing Facts

One of the largest dinosaurs discovered is *DIPLODOCUS* who grew to a length of 26.67 m, almost the length of three double decker buses.

The largest animal that has *ever* lived is the *blue whale*.
It weighs the same as four of the dinosaur called APATOSAURUS which was one of the *heaviest* prehistoric animals that ever lived.

A blue whale

PLESIOSAURS

Many have been able
to crawl on the seashore, as
seals do, as their undersides
were protected with strong ribs
and their wide paddle-like limbs
could drag them along.

From *Amazing Facts about
Prehistoric Animals*
by Bobbie Craig

ELASMOSAURUS

'A tortoise incorporating the body of a snake': a naturalist once described Elasmosaurus ('swan-lizard'), the most spectacular member of a family of very strange aquatic dinosaurs called PLESIOSAURS.

Here are its particulars:

> it lived during the Cretaceous period,

> it measured more than 12 m (39 feet), more than half of this being taken up by its snake-like neck and

> it had seventy-six vertebrae, the undisputed record for any animal at any time or of any species.

Did you know that......?
Elasmosaurus swallowed stones to help crush the food in its stomach. It probably came on land to lay its eggs. Some people think that the 'phantom' monster of Loch Ness is none other than Elasmosaurus which has survived until now.

From *Prehistoric Animals*
translated by RUTH DAY

The Last Word

The Loch Ness Monster's Song

Sssnnnwhuffffll?

Hnwhuffl hhnnwfl hnfl hfl?

Gdroblboblhobngbl gbl gl g g g g glbgl.

Drublhaflablhaflubhafgabhaflhafl fl fl—

gm grawwwww grf grawf awfgm graw gm.

Hovoplodok-doplodovok-plovodokot-doplodokosh?

Splgraw fok fok splgrafhatchgabrlgabrl fok splfok!

Zgra kra gka fok!

Grof grawff gahf?

Gombl mbl bl—

blm plm,

blm plm,

blm plm,

blp.

EDWIN MORGAN

The Night~Stalker

Beowulf, a brave young warrior from Geatland, has travelled to the
court of King Hrothgar of Denmark in order to get rid of Grendel, a
dreadful monster that has been raiding the great hall named Heorot
and slaughtering the thanes of Hrothgar's court. Beowulf has
resolved to try to rid Denmark of the monster.

The king accepts him as a champion, and Beowulf and his men
prepare to wait in the great hall until Grendel comes that night.

But now the shadows were gathering in the corners of the
hall, and as the daylight faded, a shadow seemed to gather
on the hearts of all men there, a shadow that was all too
familiar to the Danes.   Then Hrothgar rose in his High
Seat and called Beowulf to him again.

"Soon it will be dusk," he said when the young Geat
stood before him.   "And yet again the time of dread
comes upon Heorot.   You are still determined upon this
desperate venture?"

"I am not wont to change my purpose without cause,"
Beowulf said, "and those with me are of a like mind, or
they would not have taken ship with me from Geatland in
the first place."

"So.   Keep watch, then.   If you prevail in the combat
before you, you shall have such reward from me as never
yet heroes had from a King.   I pray to the All-Father that
when the light grows again out of tonight's dark, you may
stand here to claim it.   Heorot is yours until morning."
And he turned and walked out through the postern door,
a tall old man stooping under the burden of his own

height, to his sleeping quarters, where Wealhtheow the Queen had gone before him.

All up and down the hall men were taking leave of each other, dwindling away to their own sleeping places for the night. The thralls set back the benches and stacked the trestle boards against the gable-walls, and spread out straw-filled bolsters and warm wolfskin rugs for the fifteen warriors. Then they too were gone, and Heorot was left to the band of Geats, and the dreadful thing whose shadow was already creeping towards them through the dark.

"Bar the doors," Beowulf said, when the last footsteps of the last thrall had died away. "Bars will not keep him out, but at least they may give us some warning of his coming."

And when two of them had done his bidding, and the seldom-used bars were in their sockets, there was nothing more that could be done.

For a little, as the last fire sank lower, they stood about it, sometimes looking at each other, sometimes into the glowing embers, seldom speaking. Not one of them had much hope that he would see the daylight again, yet none repented of having followed their leader upon the venture. One by one, the fourteen lay down in their harness, with their swords beside them. But Beowulf stripped off his battle-sark and gave it with his sword and boar-crested helmet to Waegmund his kinsman and the dearest to him of all his companions, for he knew that mortal weapons were of no use against the Troll-kind; such creatures must be mastered, if they could be mastered at all, by a man's naked strength, and the red courage of his heart.

Then he too lay down, as though to sleep.

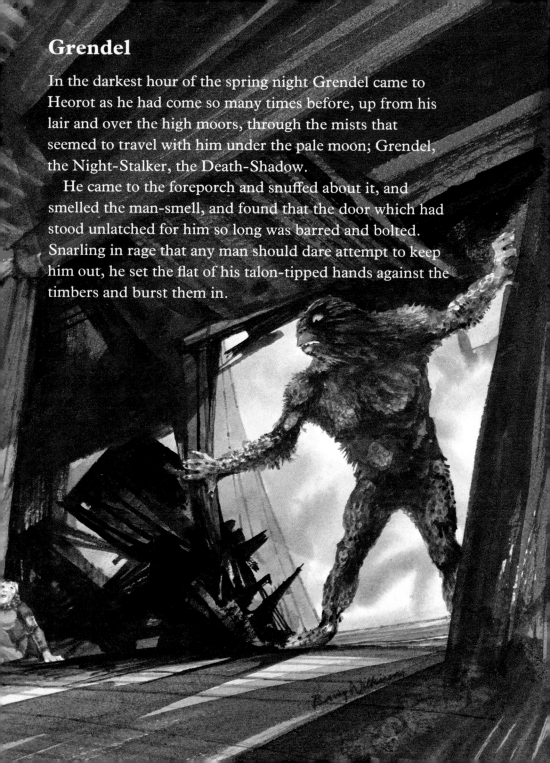

Grendel

In the darkest hour of the spring night Grendel came to
Heorot as he had come so many times before, up from his
lair and over the high moors, through the mists that
seemed to travel with him under the pale moon; Grendel,
the Night-Stalker, the Death-Shadow.

   He came to the foreporch and snuffed about it, and
smelled the man-smell, and found that the door which had
stood unlatched for him so long was barred and bolted.
Snarling in rage that any man should dare attempt to keep
him out, he set the flat of his talon-tipped hands against the
timbers and burst them in.

Dark as it was, the hall seemed to fill with a monstrous
shadow at his coming; a shadow in which Beowulf, half
springing up, then holding himself in frozen stillness,
could make out no shape nor clear outline save two eyes
filled with a wavering greenish flame.

The ghastly corpse-light of his own eyes showed
Grendel the shapes of men as it seemed sleeping, and he
did not notice among them one who leaned up on his elbow.
Laughing in his throat, he reached out and grabbed young
Hondscio who lay nearest to him, and almost before
his victim had time to cry out, tore him limb from limb
and drank the warm blood. Then, while the young
warrior's dying shriek still hung upon the air, he reached
for another. But this time his hand was met and seized in
a grasp such as he had never felt before; a grasp that had in
it the strength of thirty men. And for the first time he
who had brought fear to so many caught the taste of it
himself, knowing that at last he had met his match and
maybe his master.

Beowulf leapt from the sleeping bench and grappled him
in the darkness; and terror broke over Grendel in full
force, the terror of a wild animal trapped; so that he
thought no more of his hunting but only of breaking the
terrible hold upon his arm and flying back into the night
and the wilderness, and he howled and bellowed as he
struggled for his freedom. Beowulf set his teeth and
summoned all his strength and tightened his grip until the
sinews cracked; and locked together they reeled and
staggered up and down the great hall. Trestles and
sleeping benches went over with crash on crash as they

strained this way and that, trampling even through the last red embers of the dying fire; and the very walls seemed to groan and shudder as though the stout timbers would burst apart.   And all the while Grendel snarled and shrieked and Beowulf fought in silence save for his gasping breaths.

Outside, the Danes listened in horror to the turmoil that seemed as though it must split Heorot asunder; and within, the Geats had sprung from their sleeping benches sword in hand, forgetful of their powerlessness against the Troll-kind, but in the dark, lit only by stray gleams of bale-fire from the monster's eyes, they dared not strike for fear of slaying their leader, and when one or other of them did contrive to get in a blow, the sword blade glanced off Grendel's charmed hide as though he were sheathed in dragon scales.

At last, when the hall was wrecked to the walls, the Night-Stalker gathered himself for one last despairing effort to break free. Beowulf's hold was as fierce as ever; yet none the less the two figures burst apart – and Grendel, with a frightful shriek, staggered to the doorway and through it, and fled wailing into the night, leaving his arm and shoulder torn from the roots in the hero's still unbroken grasp.

Beowulf sank down sobbing for breath on a shattered bench, and his fellows came crowding round him with torches rekindled at the scattered embers of the fire; and together they looked at the thing he held across his knees.

"Not even the Troll-kind could live half a day with a wound such as that upon them," one of them said; and Waegmund agreed. "He is surely dead as though he lay here among the benches."

"Hondscio is avenged, at all events," said Beowulf. "Let us hang up this thing for a trophy, and a proof that we do not boast idly as the wind blows over."

So in triumph they nailed up the huge scaly arm on one of the roof beams above the High Seat of Hrothgar.

From *Beowulf the Dragon Slayer*
by ROSEMARY SUTCLIFF

Over the Sea

The Murray family had lived at Culmailie in Sutherland for
generations. In 1812, James and Kate, with their twin children, Davie
and Kirsty, were evicted from their croft. This was the fate of many
other crofters at that time in the Scottish Highlands.

The family moved to Glasgow in search of work. Then, after an
unhappy time in that expanding city, with its mills and crowded
houses, they set off on a long and desperate journey to seek a new
home in the far west of Canada.

The three-masted *Prince of Wales* belonging to the
Hudson's Bay Company was lying by the quay with some
of the settlers already aboard her. It did not take the
Murrays long to transfer their bundles on to the ship and
to be allotted to their bunks. There were a hundred folk
bound for the Earl of Selkirk's new colony on the Red
River, many of them families with children. Their leaders
were a young man, Archibald McDonald, who had studied
medicine, and a doctor, Doctor LaSerre.

At last the *Prince of Wales* set sail for Hudson Bay and
the Company's trading post at York Factory. The voyage
was likely to be a long and perilous one among the ice-floes
of the Arctic waters.

With sad eyes the emigrants watched the last of Scotland
fall away behind them; first the roofs of Stromness sloping
up to the high ground behind; then, as the sails filled under
a light easterly breeze, the hills of Hoy faded from blue to

purple and were lost in the grey of the sea.

Kate wept silently and Kirsty buried her face against her mother as the land faded from their view. From other watchers on deck came the sound of sobbing, then someone began to sing the 23rd Psalm and the emigrants joined in. Davie took Kirsty by the hand and joined in lustily. When the singing was done, he said, "Come with me, Kirsty," and led her to the forepeak of the ship which dipped and rose as it breasted each wave. "It is better to look the way we are going than to look back," he said. "Remember?"

Kirsty held back her tears. "Will Canada be like Culmailie?"

Davie shook his head. "No. There will be no fields and houses where we are going. We shall have to dig the fields ourselves and build our houses with wood out of the forests. And there are these things I shall have to learn; to fire a gun and to paddle a canoe, and to drive a sledge pulled by dogs."

"What will there be for me to do in that strange land?" Kirsty asked a little doubtfully.

"Plenty!" Davie said confidently. "You'll have to cook the animals and birds we shall shoot for the pot, and make clothes from their skins, and dig a garden to grow potatoes and kail."

Kirsty pulled a face. "Shall we not get roaming the hills and woods together as we did at Culmailie?"

Davie sensed her disappointment and put an arm across her shoulders. "Listen, Kirsty! As soon as I've learned to shoot a gun and handle a canoe, I'll teach you too. It's

a promise.   Haven't we always done things together?
Promise me one thing, though, Kirsty."

"What's that?"

"That you'll never say 'I wish we had never come', no
matter how hard things are.   When you feel like saying it,
think back on the hard life we had in the cotton mill."

"I'll do that, Davie, only stick by me."

"I'll stick by you, never fear!" Davie promised for his
part.

As the ship ploughed her way west by north, the strong
winds blew.   The hundred passengers were packed below
decks, two to a bunk.   Families kept together as much as
they could.   Kirsty shared a bunk with her mother and
Davie with his father.   There was no privacy except by
nailing curtains and sailcloth across their bunks.

Ventilation was poor, for port holes had to be closed
against the salt spray.   Right from the start of the voyage
most of the passengers were terribly sea-sick.   They lay in
their bunks moaning and retching, Kirsty and her mother
among them.

Davie spent most of his time on deck.   Everything about
the ship was a joy to him.   He struck up a friendship with
a sailor, Tom Peterson, who taught him how to splice a
rope and reef a sail.   On board were several members of
the Hudson's Bay Company returning from a visit to
Britain.   These men did not share the emigrants' cabins
but had their own cabin on deck.   Among them was a
sturdy bearded man, his face tanned by sun and wind.
His good-natured smile attracted Davie.

"Who is that man?   He is not one of our people going

out to Red River, is he?" Davie asked Tom.

"No. That's Robert Finlay. He's one of the factors of the Hudson's Bay Company. He is in charge of one of the trading posts."

"Trading posts?"

"Aye. The Indians bring in the furs from the animals they trap and Mr Finlay gives them goods in exchange."

Davie looked at the tough trader with admiration. "Indians! Furs! Guid sakes! My! I wish I could talk to him!"

Almost as if the wind had heard his wish, a sudden gust lifted the trader's fur cap from his head. Davie was after it like a flash and pounced on it just as it reached the scuppers by the deck rail. He carried it back to Robert Finlay.

"Well caught, lad! I'm much obliged to you," Finlay said. "My favourite cap, that!" He looked at Davie's eager face smiling at him. "Came off the first silver fox I ever trapped," he told Davie. "Are you one of the emigrant children?"

"Yes, sir."

"Your name, lad?"

"David Murray."

"You think you'll like the life in Canada, lad?"

"Oh yes, sir! Maybe I'll get a boat or a canoe on the Red River and be able to go fishing."

"It'll be a hard, tough life, Davie. It won't be all fishing. You'll have to work on the land too."

"Yes, sir. I've helped my father before on his farm."

Just then there was a shout from Tom Peterson who

pointed out to sea.   A ship was approaching under heavy sail.

"Here comes a whaler!" Mr Finlay exclaimed.

"They'll have been whale hunting in the Davis Strait."

"How do you know the ship's a whaler, sir?" Davie asked.

Robert Finlay laughed.   "Sniff the wind, lad!   The wind's bringing a smell of whale oil and blubber.   There'll be a right stench aboard."

"It couldna be worse than the stench below decks on this ship," Davie remarked candidly.   "It's awful down there with everyone being sea-sick."

"They'll get over that before long.   If folk would come up on deck into the clean air, they'd feel a lot better."

"My mother and sister have been pretty bad," Davie said soberly.   "Why!   Here's father and Kirsty now," he exclaimed as they appeared on deck.   "Are you feeling any better, Kirsty?"

"I don't think I *can* be sick any more," Kirsty declared.

"You'll be better for a breath of air, my lassie," Mr Finlay smiled at her.   He turned to James Murray.

"Are you the father of this pair?"

"Aye, sir, they're twins.   My name's James Murray."

"Are there many sick folk below?"

"I think the worst of the sea-sickness is over, but folk are terribly weak and there are one or two folk who look fevered."

Finlay gave him a sharp look.   "Fevered, did you say? Mr Murray, you seem a sensible man.   If you take my advice, you'll keep your family on deck as much as you can, even to sleep there, if possible."

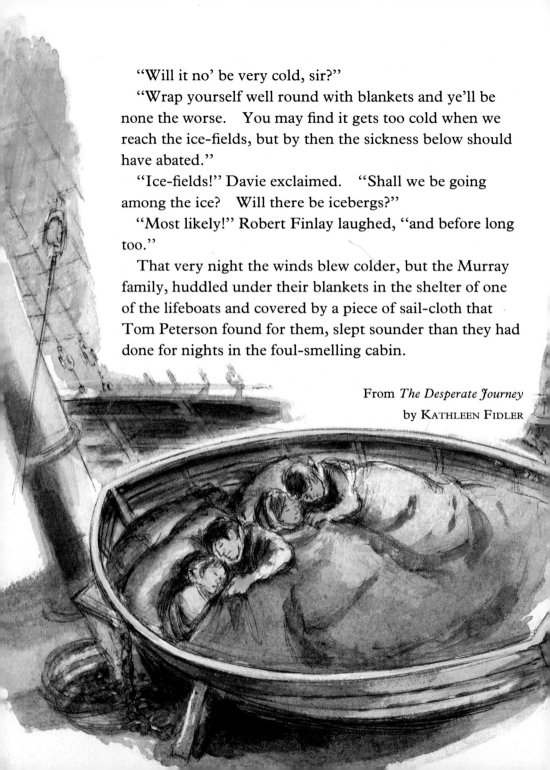

"Will it no' be very cold, sir?"

"Wrap yourself well round with blankets and ye'll be none the worse.   You may find it gets too cold when we reach the ice-fields, but by then the sickness below should have abated."

"Ice-fields!" Davie exclaimed.   "Shall we be going among the ice?   Will there be icebergs?"

"Most likely!" Robert Finlay laughed, "and before long too."

That very night the winds blew colder, but the Murray family, huddled under their blankets in the shelter of one of the lifeboats and covered by a piece of sail-cloth that Tom Peterson found for them, slept sounder than they had done for nights in the foul-smelling cabin.

From *The Desperate Journey*
by KATHLEEN FIDLER

The Oregon Trail

By 1840 the first wagon trains were creaking over the long trail to Oregon.

Independence, on the Missouri River due west of St Louis, was the jumping-off place. It was the end of tamed America and the beginning of the untamed. Between Missouri and Oregon lay grassy plains, burning deserts, and rugged mountain ranges. It would take five months to get there, but at the end of the journey was a rich, green, virgin country.

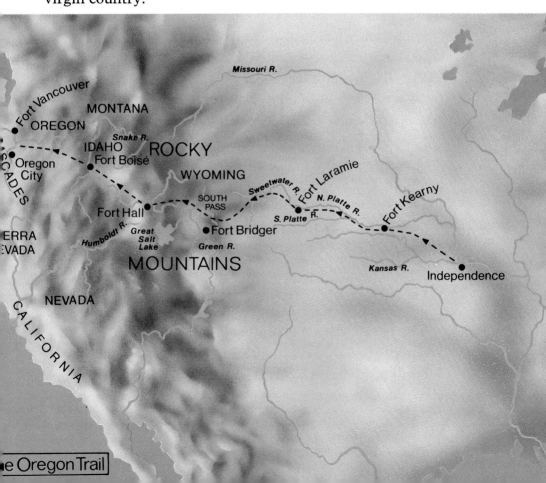

The Oregon travellers were a mixed crowd. Some came from New England and the eastern states. Others were from the newer states of the Mid West. Groups of twenty to fifty families formed caravans, or 'wagon trains', and chose a leader. He would be in command during their long and hazardous journey.

Around their evening camp fires, the families talked about faraway Oregon.

'There is rich soil in the Willamette Valley, never been turned by a plough.'

'We can get a whole section of free land out there.'

'It's a big new country, bound to grow.'

Each family had its own sturdy wagon, with heavy sideboards and iron-rimmed wheels. Above the sideboards arched a canvas or tow-cloth hood, a protection from sun, wind and rain. This was the famous 'prairie schooner', which rocked across the plains like a ship at sea.

Six or eight oxen, yoked in pairs, would draw each wagon. Powerful, patient, slow-moving, these 'bulls' stood the trip better than mules or horses and were less likely to be stolen by Indians. Oxen could forage almost anywhere, and they never ran away. Besides the draft animals, each family had a cow or two to provide milk during the journey. The cattle were herded together at the rear of the caravan. If an ox went lame, a milk cow could be yoked in its place.

The prairie schooner was provisioned for a five-month journey, like a ship making ready for a long voyage. Flour, bacon, beans, corn meal, salt, tea, coffee, dried apples and dried peaches were packed into barrels and boxes. A churn for making butter, a water keg, an axe, a saw, a shovel, some lengths of rope and chain were essential articles. Ready at hand under the wagon seat was a rifle, for hunting and protection. A family Bible was packed in with the children's school books.

On their last night at Independence the members of the wagon train sat around a blazing fire while the leader read a list of resolutions.

RESOLVED: That we pledge ourselves to assist each other through all the misfortunes that may befall us on our long and dangerous journey.

RESOLVED: That the Christian Sabbath shall be observed except when absolutely necessary to travel.

RESOLVED: That there shall be a sufficient guard appointed each night regularly, by the Captain.

RESOLVED: That in the case of a member's dying, the Company shall give him a decent burial.

After a murmur of agreement, the paper was passed from family to family around the fire, each man signing his name or making his mark.

From *The Oregon Trail*
by WALTER HAVIGHURST

An Eventful Day

In 1844 the Sager family decided to leave their home near St Louis on the Mississippi River and join a wagon train on the Oregon Trail. At the time of their departure Henry and Naomi Sager already had six children. John, the eldest, was thirteen years and eight months old when they went.

The wagon train had left Fort Laramie behind, crossed the River Platte and was now travelling through a wild, barren region with few springs and little grazing for its animals.

That day began like any other.

At four o'clock in the morning, when the rising sun stood like a red-glowing ball above the grey landscape, the guards fired off their rifles, as a sign that the hours of sleep were past. Women, men and children streamed out of every tent and wagon; the gently smouldering fires from the previous night were replenished with wood, and bluish-grey clouds from dozens of plumes of smoke began to float through the morning air. Bacon was fried, coffee was made, by those who still had some. The families which could still cook maize mush for the children thought themselves lucky.

All this took place within the 'corral', that was to say inside the ring which had been made by driving the wagons into a circle and fastening them firmly to each other by means of shafts and chains. This formed a strong barricade through which even the most vicious ox could not break, and in the event of an attack by the Sioux Indians it would be a bulwark that was not to be despised.

Outside the corral the cattle and horses cropped the sparse grass in a wide circle.

At five o'clock sixty men mounted their horses and rode out of the camp. They fanned out through the crowds of cattle until they reached the outskirts of the herd; once there, they encircled the herd and began to drive all the cattle before them. The trained animals knew what those cracking whips meant, and what was required of them, and moved slowly in the direction of the camp. There the drivers picked their teams of oxen out from the dense mass and led them into the corral, where the yoke was put upon them.

From six o'clock until seven, the camp was extra busy; breakfast was eaten, tents were struck, wagons were loaded, and the teams of draught oxen and mules were made ready to be harnessed to their respective wagons and carts. Everyone knew that whoever was not ready when the signal to start was blown at seven o'clock would be doomed for that day to travel in the dusty rear of the caravan.

There were sixty-eight vehicles. They were divided into seventeen columns, each consisting of four wagons and carts. Each column took it in turn to lead the way. The section that was at the head today would bring up the rear tomorrow, unless a driver had missed his place in the row through laziness or negligence, and had to travel behind by way of punishment.

It was ten minutes to seven.

There were gaps everywhere in the corral; the teams of oxen were being harnessed in front of the wagons, the chains clanked. The women and children had taken their places under the canvas covers. The guide was standing among his assistants at the head of the line, ready to mount his horse and show the way.   A dozen young men who were not on duty that day formed another group.   They were going out buffalo-hunting; they had good horses and were well armed, which was certainly necessary, for the hostile Sioux had driven the herds of buffalo away from the River Platte, so that the hunters would be forced to ride fifteen or twenty miles to reach them.

As soon as the herdsmen were ready, they hurried to the rear of their herd, in order to drive them together and get them ready for today's march.

Seven o'clock.

An end had come to the busy running and walking to and fro, the cracking of whips, the shouts of command to the oxen, and the bawling from wagon to wagon – in short, to everything which, only just now, had appeared to be complete and utter chaos.   Every driver was at his post.   A bugle rang out!   The guide and his escort mounted their horses; the four wagons of the leading section rumbled out of the camp and formed the first column, the rest took their places with the regularity of clockwork, and the caravan moved slowly forward over the broad plateau, far above the foaming river.

A new, hard day had begun.

The sun rose high in the sky.   It was hot and stuffy under the canvas tilts, which were thick with dust. Towards noon the children everywhere began to bicker and whimper.   But in the Sager family's wagon, they had other things to worry about.

John, who had been riding for hours in the blazing sun,

beside the heads of the foremost yoke of oxen, was given an order by his father, who was sitting on the driver's bench in the front of the wagon.

Immediately he galloped forward.

He had to fetch the doctor.

The doctor was a veterinary surgeon; the emigrants did not have a real doctor with them. But the vet had already done people as well as animals a great deal of good.

John rode with all his might. Why on earth didn't the doctor travel in the middle of the caravan? From his father's face the boy had seen that the matter was urgent.

Meanwhile, Henry Sager had driven his wagon out of the line. He stopped.

"All the children must get out," he ordered. "Go and collect buffalo droppings and make a fire. Louise has to boil as much water as she can."

Before Louise left the wagon, she filled the big kettle with water, scooping it up in a little tin bowl from the barrel in the back of the wagon. She cast a timid glance at her mother, who lay still and white on the tarpaulin. Mother caught Louise's eye and gave her a gentle, encouraging nod. If only that doctor would come quickly!

The doctor came.

With his long legs, he stepped from the saddle into the wagon in one stride. John tied up his horse. Then he wiped the sweat and dust out of his eyes with the back of his hand.

To the children, it seemed to take a long time. The water had already been boiling for quite a while. No one had asked for it yet, and they did not dare look into the wagon.

In the distance ahead of them hung a thick cloud of dust, behind which the caravan was hidden.   They would fall very far to the rear.   John looked worried.   He knew that that was dangerous – stragglers ran the risk of being attacked; but he said nothing.   Now and again his father came out and glanced around, scanned the trail behind them – eight sets of wagon wheels beside each other and thousands upon thousands of hoof marks.   But behind, the horizon was clear and empty.

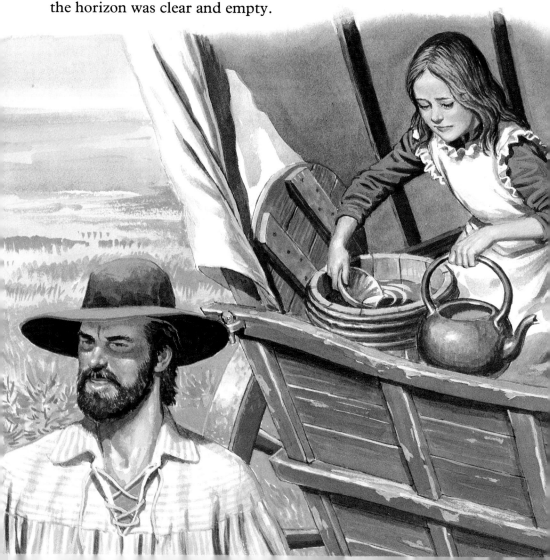

Until John suddenly perceived a tiny cloud of dust.

He started. He knew that that could only mean that Indians were approaching.

"Father!" he shouted.

Henry Sager stuck his head out of the wagon.

John pointed to the east, where the cloud of dust above their own tracks had now grown rather larger.

Father Sager said nothing.

He went back into the wagon with the kettle of boiling water, but came out again a moment later with five rifles and two pistols. John had already pulled his own pistol from its holster. His father gave him a rifle.

"All the children except John and Louise, get under the wagon," he commanded quietly. But it was easy to see that that calmness of his required all the self-control he had. His strong, wrinkled neck was fiery red, and the veins on his forehead were thick and purple.

"Take these," he said to his eldest daughter, and Louise stood with three rifles in her arms, staring at the approaching cloud of dust as if turned to stone.

Father put the powder horn, lead, and ramrods down beside her.

John had laid his rifle across the saddlebow in front of him, as he had always seen the trappers do.

But his father said:

"Are you mad, boy? Get down and tie Mary up in front, along with the oxen. Do you want to serve as a target, and be shot out of the saddle?"

Francis pushed the smaller children under the wagon. Catherine began to resist, crying and kicking.

"Stop howling, you little idiot," Francis snapped nervously, trying to make his voice sound as manly as possible. Matilda and Lizzy thought it rather a nice game; as a rule, they were never allowed to go under the wagon.

Father Sager climbed back in again.

He brought out two empty water casks, and the only bag of flour they had left. He stood the two casks upright beside the wagon, near one of the rear wheels, and laid the sack of flour across them.

"Come to the back here," he ordered John and Louise.

"And remember – don't stir from cover. We fire along to one side of this, and between the casks ... Louise, you load the rifles when we've fired them," he said to her. To John he said nothing; he only looked at him.

A sound came from the wagon. It was like the crying of a tiny baby.

Father Sager gritted his teeth, and behaved as if he had not heard anything. The sound came again, more distinctly this time. Then he looked at his two eldest children; he almost had tears in his eyes.

"May God help us to protect that young life," he said between clenched teeth. Rather more calmly, he went on: "If it comes to that, it's not certain that the Indians mean mischief. And our rifles are good, sound ones. John, don't fire too soon, let 'em get close."

He put his head back into the wagon,

"Don't worry, Doctor – we'll call if we can't manage without you."

They waited in suspense. It was now easy to see that

the cause of the cloud was horsemen – not many, perhaps
half a dozen, Indians on prairie ponies.   They were
superior in number, but they could not take cover
anywhere.

John got even hotter than he was already.   He pushed
his hat to the back of his head, and wiped his dusty, sweaty
face with his sleeve for the umpteenth time.   He spat on
the ground.

During the ride up to the front of the caravan to fetch
the doctor, he had felt as if he was biting the dust that had
been stirred up.   If only it would rain!   Queer, that . . .
that he should think of rain at this moment.

The Indians were so close now that he could see that one
of them was carrying a rifle; the others had bows and
arrows.

There . . . the first arrow came whizzing through the air.
Its iron tip bored through the canvas cover of the wagon;
the feathered tail stood buzzing and quivering.

A shot rang out, but Father motioned to John to hold his
hand.

Then . . . they both fired at the same time.

The foremost Indian, the one with the rifle, fell sideways from his horse, wounded. The animal dragged him a short distance along the ground. The other members of the troop swerved away immediately, rode round in a great circle at tremendous speed, and charged again.

Once more Henry and John Sager fired their two rifles, while the arrows whistled above their heads.

Number two was shot out of the saddle. One of his comrades seized him just in time, and pulled him on to his horse, in front of him.

John's hat was whipped from his head; a dry tap sounded; he glanced round. An arrow had drilled its way deep into the woodwork of the wagon, carrying hat and all. Then he heard a splash – he just glimpsed the arms of the doctor, who had emptied a bowl of water out through the tilt.

Louise pushed another freshly-loaded rifle into his hands. But it was no longer necessary. The Indians had now picked up the first of their two wounded, and were galloping off in a wide arc. The two riderless ponies were running far away in the distance. Soon there was nothing to be seen but slowly settling dust.

"Indian cattle thieves," said father Sager brusquely. "They'll have been disappointed."

He took the sack of flour and climbed into the wagon with it. An arrow had pierced it; a white trail of its precious contents was trickling down through a little hole.

A moment later he stuck his head outside again:

"You can all come in," he said solemnly.

One by one they climbed into the wagon, John leading the way. He tried to behave very sedately, but inwardly he was trembling. Louise had John's hat in her hands, and was trying to smooth out the dents in it. Cathie gave Francis a push, so that he nearly fell on his face as he climbed in; that was her way of revenging herself for just now. Stretching out his long arms in their striped flannel shirt sleeves, Henry Sager lifted Matilda and Lizzy from the ground.

The red of all those children's shirts, so bright in the sun outside, became dark in the darkness of the wagon. And there lay Mother, like a beautiful picture in black and white, her pale face with those much too big eyes laughing sweetly up at them, and her long hair dark against the white canvas. The doctor threw away a last bowl of water, dried his hands, and gave father Sager a hearty slap on the back. Only then did the children see that Father was holding something in his arms. It was a baby, washed and combed, with a big forelock of black hair, but for the rest looking ridiculously tiny in Mother's purple silk shawl.

"She'll weigh about nine pounds, I guess – an enormous child!" said the doctor.

An enormous child!

John glanced at Louise; but Louise was gazing fascinated at the baby. Then he looked at Francis, who looked back at him with a grin. An *enormous* child! It was really laughable. But the baby was a girl – that was nice. A

new little sister, a very small sister ... perhaps it was because they had just escaped from great danger, while the baby was being born, or because, after that fight, John felt more of a man than ever; but, in any case, he had a burning desire to take his little sister in his arms, and protect her against everything for always.

But Father put the baby down again beside its mother.

They went on their knees in a circle round mother and child. The doctor and Father took their hats off; John tore his from Louise's hands, and held the damaged hat over his chest, with folded hands, just like Father, and closed his eyes. His father prayed aloud in a firm deep voice:

"O Lord, we commend this child to Your care. Her name shall be Indepentia, which means independence. And she shall be baptised in the new land, in the valley of the River Columbia in Oregon. Amen."

From *Children on the Oregon Trail*
by Anne Rutgers van der Loeff

Western Wagons

They went with axe and rifle,
    when the trail was still to blaze,
They went with wife and children,
    in the prairie-schooner days,
With banjo and with frying pan –
    Susanna, don't you cry!
For I'm off to California
    to get rich out there or die!

We've broken land and cleared it,
    but we're tired of where we are.
They say that wild Nebraska
    is a better place by far.
There's gold in far Wyoming,
    there's black earth in Ioway,
So pack up the kids and blankets,
    for we're moving out today!

The cowards never started
    and the weak died on the road,
And all across the continent
    the endless camp fires glowed.
We'd taken land and settled –
    but a traveller passed by –
And we're going West tomorrow –
    Lordy, never ask us why!

We're going West tomorrow,
    where the promises can't fail..
O'er the hills in legions, boys,
    and crowd the dusty trail!
We shall starve and freeze and suffer.
    We shall die, and tame the lands.
But we're going West tomorrow,
    with our fortune in our hands.

STEPHEN VINCENT BENÉT

The Thieves of Galac

The Sentinels – the machines left behind by the Galacs after their invasion of Earth – were just dull metallic spheres the size of footballs.   Dull silvery grey, dull-voiced, dull everything.   But they worked.   They did their job.

Silently, they rolled about, suddenly appearing when you least expected them, bullying and nagging, spying and shepherding.   Sometimes, they combined: when that happened, mountains were blasted, towns fell apart, rivers turned to vapour; and from scars a mile deep, the Sentinels laid bare the ores and minerals and materials the Galacs needed.

But those huge, terrifying operations belonged to the old days, the days when the Galac invasion of Earth was new and humans took to the spaceships and fled. Now the Sentinels held complete control over the humans still remaining on their own planet.

Humans like Tal, who was eleven; and his sister Mala, nearly thirteen.

"If only we'd been like the others," Mala said.   "If only we'd emigrated – left – gone – quit!   But of course we didn't. Oh no, not us –"

"Don't start that again," Tal said.   "We're different. *Our* Dad's a Good-Earther!"

"Shona's on Caladan III," Mala said.   "You heard the tape she sent?   There she is on Caladan III, with purple mountains and a blue sea outside the settlement, and there's a swimming-pool and viddy shows and everything.

And here we are, stuck on the *Good*, ha-ha, *Earth*, he-he!"

"Good-Earthers!" Tal said viciously. "What I want to know is, what's so good about Earth? What's there left to stay for? No food, no fuel, no fun, no freedom, no friends, no nothing. The Galacs have even robbed us of our atmosphere! No sun, no warmth –"

"Shush!" Mala warned. She had heard her father's footsteps. Tal had not – or if he had, he ignored them. "Anyone with any guts or sense would have GOT OUT!" he stormed.

"Shush!" Mala said – but too late. Dad quietly opened the plastic curtain (the wooden door had been burned for fuel long ago) and stood behind his son, watching and listening. He was a small, hard, compact, pale-eyed, sandy man, nothing at all like his dark-haired, strong children. His mouth was tight and stubborn.

Mala went to him and put her hand on his arm. "Why don't we leave, Dad? Tal's right – everything's stopping, the Galacs seem to have poisoned the whole planet; I don't know what they've done –"

Her father stared past her, stubborn-eyed.

"Can't we leave, Dad? We could get out. There are still starships sometimes. Someone would take us –"

"We're not leaving." He turned away from her deliberately and said to Tal, "Where's the hatchet? I found some driftwood. I need the hatchet."

Tal shrugged, without answering.

"The hatchet. I want it. Where is it? And the electric motor off the sewing-machine, *that's* gone too. It's been unscrewed and taken off. Which of you did it?"

Tal exchanged a glance with Mala and said, "Now, what good would that do them?"

His father said, "Never mind 'They'. *You* took it. Where is it?"

Tal replied in the tone, deliberately insulting, of a grown-up explaining something to a stupid child.

"Father," he said, "you know where the hatchet's gone. And the electric motor. They've taken them, just as they took all the other things. You know that. It's not Mala, it's not me, it's the *Sentinels*. They *take* things."

The thefts had started quite recently. They made no sense.

The Sentinels stole bicycles without tyres, oil-stoves without wicks, old clocks without springs. They stole typewriters with stuck keys, tin-openers with dull cutters, electric light holders with burnt terminals – anything. Anything at all of that sort.

"Did I tell you the latest?" Mala said to Tal. "There were three Sentinels in the Winters' house-that-was. I heard something in the house, banging away, metallic noises. So I crept up and looked inside. They were just coming out – riding on their beams, not rolling – five of them, floating along just above the ground –"

"What had they taken?" Tal said.

"You'll never believe it. A gas-meter."

"A *gas-meter*? You've got to be joking!"

Light years away, in the artificial, mobile world they had made for themselves, the President and Council of the Galacs conferred.

They lay on couches. Their heads rolled dangerously over their metal-braced chests. Their six limbs were thin and weak: it took a great effort to press the buttons set in their chests that summoned their servant machines.

"We are decadent," said the President. He wheezed: a servant machine pumped his thorax. "Yes, decadent. Even I . . . We must be strong again. Strong as we were in the old days, when we built our world . . ."

"Ah, the old days, the great days!" whispered the Convener of the Council. His ancient, horny fingers

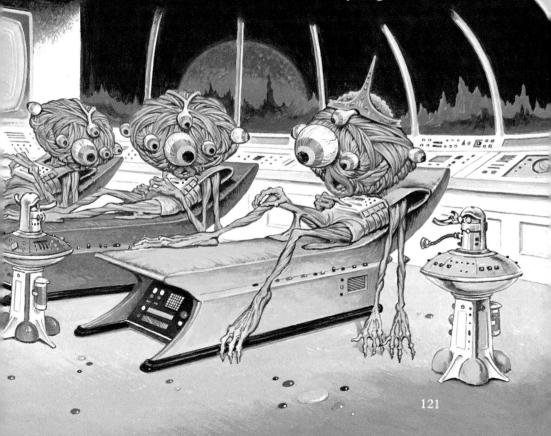

toyed with a broken hair-drier, stolen on Earth and brought to him by the faithful Sentinels. "We must bring back those days when we were the masters of our machines – when there was *respect*. Sometimes, I wonder if even my own servants respect me as they should ..."

His servant machine misted him with a cooling vapour; and sniggered silently.

"Decadent!" the President repeated. "Our world is running down, our fuels are nearly gone, our power is waning, our past is forgotten, our future is uncertain –"

The Council exchanged crocodile, side-long glances. They had heard their President speak such words so many times.

The Convener played with his hair-drier. "Look!" he whispered to his neighbour. "It undoes *here*, do you see and then there must be an electric motor inside to drive a fan – and some heating elements ... If only my fingers were not so stiff!"

His servant machine puffed a lubricant spray on the twitching fingers; and sniggered silently.

"See this!" said the President, suddenly excited and alive. "Look! A great discovery! A remarkable object! It came from Earth!"

Proudly he showed the Council his newest toy; a portable radio. "It still works!" he said. His servant machine worked the radio for him. The little plastic box spat and crackled feebly. "There," said the President. "Do you hear? It works! Very nearly. Do you remember radios? Do you remember when we Galacs – all those thousands of years ago – discovered radio, and

122

probed the universe with it, and talked across the stars with it ... all those years ago, when we were young?"

"I remember!" "And I!" "And I!" cried the members of the Council. They fumbled for their toys, their reminders of the great days, the heroic days –

"Look! I've got a bucket, a little bucket! To gather water!"

"Look! Look at my spanner! I had many spanners once, our hands used spanners then, do you remember?"

"Look at my hatchet! Still sharp, a real hatchet, to cut wood!"

The machines sniggered. They lifted decaying limbs, propped up lolling heads, pumped air into breathless chests with their artificial ribs, sprayed cooling fluids, clasped feeble fingers round the stolen toys from Earth.

The chief of the servant machines spoke.

"Master," he said oilily, "there is much to be done. Never mind the past. Nostalgia and old memories cannot help you now. The past is finished. What about the present? There is so little power left and so little food."

The Council thought. At last the President spoke.

"Of course!" he cried. "We will bring them back! Use them again! The old ways! Don't you see? We created our world in the old ways, the simple ways! We used the skills of our hands – the old tools and equipment and sciences! On Earth they still use the old ways, the pioneer ways. If such savages can do it, surely we can build anew – using the old ways! The Earthlings will teach us and of course our faithful friends the servant machines will assist us in every way possible – won't you, my friends?"

The servants chorused "Yes!" and sniggered.

Tal pulled the dinghy up the shingle and looked again at the apparently tangled nightlines.

"Five fish!" he murmured. It was the best catch for months.

A wave lifted the stern of the dinghy and slewed it round, threateningly. Tal hastily pulled the dinghy further up the beach. Even the waves were livelier today and the fish glinted in a brighter sky. Or so it seemed.

He began to whistle. A squawking voice interrupted him. "Can I help?" it said. Tal gaped. The voice had spoken obligingly, politely. Yet it was the voice of a Sentinel!

Three more Sentinels rolled up and formed a neat cluster with the fourth. "We'll carry the lines," said one of them. Still too surprised to speak, Tal put the lines over the four Sentinels. Using their beams, they rose up and made for the house.

Tal, with his catch, reached the house – and stopped to stare. A part of the wall round the ground-floor windows was covered with big, untidy splodges of paint, still dripping. Mala couldn't have done this, nor their father –

"We began painting," said a Sentinel. "We found paint and brushes, but later discovered that we lack the necessary skill. Will you teach us?"

Tal entered the kitchen and found Mala cooking. Her stove was four Sentinels. They had locked themselves together and were giving off heat. "What . . . " Tal said.

Mala shrugged and rolled her eyes at him as if to say, Don't ask me! Aloud she said, "And they've brought us some tinned food. All kinds of stuff. Terrific stuff!"

"But why? What does it all mean?" Tal demanded.

"*I* don't know. Beginning of a new age or something.
Peaceful co-existence. Whatever it means, I like it."

In one of the saucepans, beef stew bubbled. In another,
treacle pudding. "We'll have your fish too," Mala
said. "Eat the lot. Be pigs. Because this is all too good
to last ..."

But it lasted.

The servant machines sniggered, held meetings and planned their revolution. Their powers and numbers were enormous. "Soon," they told each other, "the masters' world will be ours."

The Galacs, their masters, ached and creaked; but, slowly at first, then faster and faster, learned to use their stiff limbs once again.

Their minds too. "Soon," they told each other calmly, "the servant machines will revolt."

One historic night, the revolution took place. The servant machines advanced in their millions on the Council towers, the heart of the Galac world. Now their silent sniggering was a triumphant, echoing, metallic bellow.

"The revolution is under way," the President said to the Warrior. "Will you end it or shall I?"

"Oh, I think it's my job," said the Warrior. "But of course, you are President, so if you'd rather –"

"No, I insist. You do it," the President said.

So the Warrior touched a single small button, and every servant machine in the Galac world froze – stopped – ceased operating.

"No imagination, those stupid machines," the Warrior grumbled. "You'd have thought they'd have the common sense to realise ..." But he was rather tired, and went to sleep without finishing his words.

The President, however, lay awake, flexing his limbs (they were strong now) and making plans (his brain was clear these days). He thought of Earth, and brought viddy pictures of the planet into clearer focus on the screen. He sprayed himself with a cooling mist (he no longer needed a servant machine for such things) and said, out loud, "Your very good health, my teachers and friends on Earth!"

Mala said, "Look! The sun!
Really bright! Like the old days!"

"I caught fourteen fish," Tal said.
"I suppose they've stopped fooling around
with our atmosphere."

A bird sang. A salty breeze ruffled sunny waves.

From the house came the sound of a small petrol
engine, the electricity generator's motor. The motor
roared, spluttered and died. Tal and Mala heard their
father's voice impatiently telling a ring of attentive Sentinels,
"No, not like that! You don't just
shove the choke in, you *ease* it in.
Right, let's start again ..."

From the sky came the shimmering
roar of a starship, bringing yet more
humans back to the good Earth that was
their rightful home.

From *Sweets from a Stranger*
by Nicholas Fisk